MEDIEVAL MONASTICISM

A SELECT BIBLIOGRAPHY

TORONTO MEDIEVAL BIBLIOGRAPHIES 6

General Editor: John Leyerle

Published in Association with
the Centre for Medieval Studies, University of Toronto
by University of Toronto Press

GILES CONSTABLE

Medieval Monasticism

A SELECT BIBLIOGRAPHY

UNIVERSITY OF TORONTO PRESS
Toronto and Buffalo

© University of Toronto Press 1976
Toronto and Buffalo
Printed in Canada
Reprinted 1977

Giles Constable is currently H.C. Lea Professor of Medieval History
at Harvard University.

This bibliography was originally planned for publication in 1975;
for technical reasons publication was not possible before early 1976.

Library of Congress Cataloging in Publication Data

Constable, Giles
   Medieval monasticism
   (Toronto medieval bibliographies; no 6)
   Includes index.
   1 Monasticism and religious orders – Middle Ages,
   600-1500 – Bibliography. I Title.   II Series.
   Z7839.C8 [BX2470]   016.255'009'02   75-42284
   ISBN 0-8020-2200-6
   ISBN 0-8020-6280-6 pbk

CN ISSN 0082-5042

Editor's Preface

The study of the Middle Ages has been developed chiefly within university departments such as English or History. This pattern is increasingly being supplemented by an interdisciplinary approach in which the plan of work is shaped to fit the subject studied. The difference of approach is between Chaucer the English poet and Chaucer the civil servant of London attached to the court of Richard II, a man interested in the Ptolemaic universe and widely read in Latin, French, and Italian. Interdisciplinary programs tend to lead readers into areas relatively unfamiliar to them where critical bibliographies prepared with careful selectivity by an expert are essential. The Centre for Medieval Studies at the University of Toronto takes such an interdisciplinary approach to the Middle Ages, and the need for selective bibliographies has become apparent in our work. The Centre has undertaken to meet this need by sponsoring the Toronto Medieval Bibliographies.

In his valuable guide, *Serial Bibliographies for Medieval Studies*,* Richard H. Rouse describes 283 bibliographies; the number is surprisingly large and indicates the considerable effort now being made to provide inclusive lists of items relevant to medieval studies. The total amount in print is already vast; for one unfamiliar with a subject, significant work is difficult to locate and the problem grows worse with each year's output. The reader may well say, like the throng in *Piers Plowman* seeking the way to *Treuthe*, 'This were a wikked way but who-so hadde a gyde' (B.vi.1). The Toronto Medieval Bibliographies are meant to be such guides; each title is prepared by an expert and gives directions to important work in the subject.

*Publications of the Center for Medieval and Renaissance Studies 3, University of California, Los Angeles (Berkeley and Los Angeles 1969)

Each volume gives a list of works selected with three specific aims. One is to aid students who are relatively new to the area of study, for example Medieval Celtic Literature. Another is to guide more advanced readers in a subject where they have had little formal training, for example Medieval Rhetoric or Monasticism; and the third is to assist new libraries in forming a basic collection in the subject presented. Individual compilers are given scope to organize a presentation that they judge will best suit their subject and also to make brief critical comments as they think fit. Clarity and usefulness of a volume are preferred over any demand for exact uniformity from one volume to another.

This book, *Medieval Monasticism*, has been published with the help of a grant from the Humanities Research Council of Canada, using funds provided by the Canada Council, whose support is acknowledged with thanks.

Toronto, June 1975

JL

Contents

Western Monasticism: Chronological 28

Western Monasticism: Special Topics 51

Western Monasticism: Regional 62

Economy 107

Rules and Customs 119

The Status of Monks 123

Monastic Ideals and Spirituality 146

Author's Preface

Scope

The purpose of this bibliography is to provide a guide to the secondary literature on Christian monasticism from its origins to the end of the Middle Ages for students and scholars who are familiar with the principal western European languages. While some preference has been given to works in English, and only translations into English are indicated, many of the titles are in French, German, Italian, Latin, and Spanish.[1] This limitation inevitably bears hard on certain regions, especially in the East and in Scandinavia; and even elsewhere some useful works have been omitted because they are in other languages. A number of others have been omitted because they were unavailable, since except for a very few titles marked 'Not seen' all of the works cited here have been personally inspected. Experience has shown that many titles cited in bibliographies are either unfindable or, occasionally, non-existent, being the result either of mistakes or of over-optimistic anticipation of works which never appeared. Even those few titles marked 'Not seen' have all been verified from the catalogues of major libraries, and some works which might otherwise have been included have doubtless been overlooked owing to their unavailability.[2] Even

---

1 Omitting a few works not easily classified, about 36 per cent are in French, 30 per cent in German, 19 per cent in English, 9 per cent in Italian, and 3 per cent each in Latin and Spanish. Leclercq and Berlière between them account for 44 of the French titles. The other 'two-figure' scholars are Penco (14), Hofmeister (13), Knowles (10), and Hilpisch (10), with Lesne (9) and Gougaud (8) not far behind. Both Hallinger and Schreiber have 7 each.
2 The rarity, for instance, of the *Rivista storica benedettina* in the United States has made it difficult to include references to its contents.

as it is, a number of old and rare books and periodicals have been included, which the average reader may find hard to locate; but I can guarantee that they all exist and are evidence of the wide geographical and chronological distribution of work done on medieval monasticism.[3]

The selection and arrangement of entries in any bibliography implies a particular vision and interpretation of the subject, with which the reader should be familiar, and two points should be made with regard to this one. 1) The term monasticism is used here to refer to any way of life inspired by a desire to leave the world and to seek salvation, either alone or with others, by consecration to God. It therefore includes hermits, recluses, and many types of canons but not members of the mendicant, military, and other orders for whom work in the world was an essential part of their religious vocation. This omission may surprise some scholars, but it is justified by the terminological distinction, which survives in English, between *monachus* (monk) and *frater* (friar). 2) The net has been thrown wide in an effort to touch on every period and aspect of monasticism, and some works on familiar topics have therefore been omitted in order to make room for works, some of them brief and relatively insignificant, on less well-worked themes. Among the categories of works of which many have been excluded are (a) general works on ecclesiastical and intellectual history (such as those of H. O. Taylor and J. de Ghellinck), unless they include significant special sections on monasticism; (b) biographies of all but a few exceptionally important monks, who influenced more than one house; and (c) works on individual houses, except for heads of orders and centres of reform.[4] Collective volumes on general monastic topics have been included but not, with a few exceptions, on single houses. In recent years commemorative volumes in honour of the foundation of a monastery or of

3 Again with a few omissions, the titles break down chronologically into 13 from the 17th century — a great period of monastic historiography —, 11 from the 18th, 56 from the 19th, 57 from the 1900s, 58 from the 1910s, 96 from the 1920s, 97 from the 1930s, 103 from the 1940s, 221 from the 1950s, 247 from the 1960s, and 66 from the 1970s. These figures reflect not only the preference given here to more recent works but also the growth in interest in monastic history in the last twenty-five years.

4 For biographies and studies of individual houses, good guides are available in Chevalier 1 and Cottineau 2, and, for later works, in the serial bibliographies **19-20**.

some notable event in its history have become increasingly popular. The earliest example of this type of publication known to me is the *Millénaire de Cluny* published in 1910, and their numbers have multiplied since the Second World War. Another volume for Cluny appeared in 1950 (**206**), and subsequently similar volumes have been published for Vallombrosa in 1951; Amorbach and Nonantola in 1953; Gladbach and Jumièges in 1955; Maria-Laach, Ste Fare (**319**), and Weingarten in 1956; Fécamp, Le Bec, and St Germain-des-Prés in 1959; Jouarre in 1961; St Riquier in 1962; Corbie, Mt Athos (**122**), Münsterschwarzach, and Pomposa in 1963; Ellwangen, Lorsch, Moissac, and Ottobeuren in 1964; Metten in 1965; Payerne and St Victor at Marseille in 1966; Mont St-Michel and St Peter at Perugia in 1967; Neustadt, Neuzelle, and St Laurence at Liège in 1968. Almost all of these, and others, contain useful contributions but have been excluded here as being of primarily local interest.

These rules have not been observed rigidly. Several works on individual houses, for instance, have been included for regions for which there is a lack of other suitable works and in the area of economic and constitutional history, where much of the best recent work has been in the form of detailed local studies. The dangers of generalization in the study of monastic history, as Dom Dubois has recently stressed (**202**), are perhaps even greater than those of specialization, since every monastery has its own history, and many sweeping statements about medieval monasticism are based on inadequate knowledge. The best introduction to the field, therefore, is often through a local study, biography, or translation of an original source. Particular attention should be drawn to the series of translations of sources on early monasticism in Egypt in the *Corpus scriptorum christianorum orientalium* and, for monasticism in the West, in Nelson's *Medieval Classics* (now the *Oxford Medieval Texts*), which include the *Chronicle of Jocelin of Brakelond*, Walter Daniel's *Life of Aelred of Rievaulx*, and the *Monastic Constitutions of Lanfranc*. Other biographies of which translations into English have recently appeared, and which provide a special insight into the character of medieval monasticism, are those of Odo of Cluny, Guibert of Nogent, and Christina of Markyate. Their omission here should be taken as a sign not of their unimportance or lack of interest but of the almost inexhaustible richness of the sources for the study of medieval monasticism, of which only a small fraction could be included here.

Arrangement

The arrangement by subject is intended both to indicate the range of topics covered and to help the reader find relevant titles easily. Not all works, however, fit easily under a single subject heading. Does monastic work and poverty, for instance, belong under economy or spirituality? Should the works on women in religious life, or on Byzantine monasticism, be grouped together or broken down into relevant subject classifications? In fact, in this bibliography, the former have been listed together and the latter scattered, showing that no rigid system has been followed. But the tendency has been to classify according to topic rather than to region or period, with cross-references to relevant works in other sections. And I hope that each section is sufficiently specific that works on desired subjects can be found without too great difficulty.

Within each classification or sub-classification the titles are arranged if possible by subject, going from general to specific and from early to late, or by date of publication, *not* in alphabetical order of the authors' names. In general, therefore, the most general and earliest works come first and the most specific and recent works last. Evaluative comments like 'useful' or 'revises earlier views' have on the whole been avoided in favour of factual information and brief references to other works on the title or topic in question. Occasionally, when two or more works by the same author are closely related, short, or in effect parts of a series, they are given under a single entry number.

Method of Citation

The references are in principle to the latest revised edition of each work, with the date of the first edition (or original publication of an article) given in parentheses immediately after the title and forming the basis for the chronological listing of works in order of publication.[5] The name of the author is, when possible, given in the vernacular form with the full first name and middle name or initial. I know how hard it can be to locate the

---

5 Reprints are mentioned only if they include significant new material. Occasionally reprints are called editions, even on the title-pages, but these are not mentioned here if there is no ascertainable difference from earlier printings. I may have overlooked, however, some genuinely revised editions.

work of an author when only the initials or translated form of the name are known, and Latin and other forms of names are therefore silently translated here, and full first names given, even if they do not appear in the title in question.[6] Names in religion and married names present particular problems, since the same scholar may have published under several names. Many writers today have reverted, sometimes by stages, from their religious to their baptismal names, and married women have resumed their maiden names. Monks in England especially tend to combine their baptismal and religious names, like Francis Aidan Gasquet and Edward Cuthbert Butler. The preference here is for the baptismal name, when it can be discovered, with the alternate name in brackets; but personal preferences have been followed when they are known and religious names cited when used consistently by the author.[7]

Titles are given as they appear on the title-page or on the first page of articles except that capitalization has been normalized: all major words in English, nouns in German, and proper names only in French, Italian, Latin, and Spanish. The original spellings have been preserved, as of *abbies* (for *abbeys*) in older English usage and of *th* for *t* (in *Mönchthum*, *Wirthschaft*, etc) and of *c*, *k*, *s*, and *z* (in the words for Benedictine and Cistercian) in German; but it is hard to be entirely consistent in this respect. Sub-titles have been included when they throw light on the subject of a book and have been set off from the main title by a colon in English and by a period in other languages. The names of collections and series are given (except for those sponsored by universities) only when the volumes are numbered.[8] The independent publication of offprints and collected articles from journals, sometimes with a title-page and new pagination, can be confusing,

---

6 For Dom Beaunier (408), however, I have been unable to find even an initial! For authors who consistently prefer their middle to their first names, such as J. Armitage Robinson and A. Hamilton Thompson, I have given the full middle name.
7 Hilpisch and Dimier consistently use their names in religion, but in differing forms. Hilpisch, whose baptismal name is Ferdinand, appears with Stephanus (which is used here), Stephan, and Stephen; Dimier, whose baptismal name is Joseph, with Marie-Anselme (which is used here) and Anselme. Several authors translate their names into the language in which they are writing, and it is not always easy to ascertain the correct form.
8 Not all series are consistent in their numbering, giving numbers to some volumes and not to others. Only the second and third series of the Cambridge Studies in Medieval Life and Thought are numbered.

and the original publication is preferred here unless only the separate form was known or available. The place of publication is given as on the title-page of the copy consulted, but translated into the familiar form for modern readers. A dash (-) between place-names indicates simultaneous publication; a slash (/) indicates different places of publication for the successive volumes of sets. The dates of works originally published in parts (such as 2, 39, and 40) are given from the appearance not of the first part but of the first entire volume, as on the title-page. When there is no indication of date or place of publication in the work, approximations are given in brackets (based on place of printing, date of *imprimatur*, etc). The total number of volumes in a work is indicated in Arabic numerals; a specific volume in a set, in Roman numerals. An Arabic numeral separated by a period from a Roman or Arabic numeral (or, rarely, from a date) indicates a part, usually separately paginated, of a volume or series.

Acknowledgements

I am indebted to Professors Charles Julian Bishko of the University of Virginia and Ihor Ševčenko of Harvard University for looking over the entries, respectively, on Spanish and on Byzantine monasticism and for making valuable suggestions. Dr Peter King of St Andrew's University kindly provided some entries on Scandinavian monasticism, as did Mr Desider Vikor of Harvard University on monasticism in Hungary; and Ms Leslie McCoull of the Institute of Christian and Oriental Research at the Catholic University of America helped with the section on Coptic monasticism. Samuel Cohn, Robert Sullivan, and Mary Woodward all helped with checking and proof-reading. Their assistance was made possible by a grant from the Clark-Harvard Graduate Society funds of Harvard University. My daughter also spent some valued hours with me searching for books in the library. Finally, the whole work has benefitted enormously from the careful scrutiny and many helpful suggestions of Ms Anna Burko of the Centre for Medieval Studies at the University of Toronto.

GC

Abbreviations

Anal cist	*Analecta cisterciensia* (31)
Anal praem	*Analecta praemonstratensia* (33)
Archives	Archives de la France monastique (35)
Beiträge	Beiträge zur Geschichte des alten Mönchtums und des Benediktinerordens (36)
Coll cist	*Collectanea cisterciensia* (30)
KR Abh	Kirchenrechtliche Abhandlungen (34)
N	New, nouvelle, etc (with S)
Rev bén	*Revue bénédictine* (26)
Rev d'hist ecc	*Revue d'histoire ecclésiastique* (18)
Rev Mab	*Revue Mabillon* (27)
S	Series, série, etc (also used for Folge and Reihe)
Sav-Zs, Kan Abt	*Zeitschrift der Savigny-Stiftung für Rechtsgeschichte, Kanonistische Abteilung*
Stud Ans	Studia Anselmiana (37)
Stud Mitt	*Studien und Mitteilungen zur Geschichte des Benediktinerordens und seiner Zweige* (25)
Stud mon	*Studia monastica* (24)
Zs	*Zeitschrift*
Zs für KG	*Zeitschrift für Kirchengeschichte*

MEDIEVAL MONASTICISM

PART I: REFERENCE

Bibliographies

GENERAL

1
Chevalier, Ulysse *Répertoire des sources historiques du moyen âge. Bio-bibliographie* (1877-88) 2nd ed 2 vols (Paris 1905-7)
Still useful for bibliography on individual persons.
2
Cottineau, Laurent H. *Répertoire topo-bibliographique des abbayes et prieurés* 3 vols (Mâcon 1939-70)
Vol III (prepared by Grégoire Poras) contains abbreviations and indices. Largely replaces Chevalier *Topo-bibliographie* (1894-1903) for individual houses.

CARTULARIES

3
Oesterley, Hermann *Wegweiser durch die Literatur der Urkunden Sammlungen* 2 vols (Berlin 1885-6)
Covers all Europe, with emphasis on Germany.
4
Stein, Henri *Bibliographie générale des cartulaires français ou relatifs à l'histoire de France* (Manuels de bibliographie historique 4; Paris 1907)
Cf also the lists of cartularies containing documents prior, respectively, to 1000 and 1100, in *Archivum Latinitatis medii aevi* 15 (1940) 5-24 and 22 (1953) 239-59.
5
Davis, Godfrey R. C. *Medieval Cartularies of Great Britain* (London - New York - Toronto 1958).

SPECIAL

Egypt

6

Kammerer, Winifred, Elinor M. Husselman, and Louise A. Schier *A Coptic Bibliography* (University of Michigan: General Library Publications 7; Ann Arbor 1950)
Nos 2476-2569 cover early monasticism, especially in Egypt.

Ireland

7

Kenney, James F. *The Sources for the Early History of Ireland: An Introduction and Guide ... in Two Volumes,* I: *Ecclesiastical* (New York 1929)
Covers Irish monasticism both in Ireland and on the Continent down to the twelfth century. Vol II was never published.

Benedictines

8

Kapsner, Oliver L. *A Benedictine Bibliography* (1949-50) 2nd ed 2 vols (Collegeville, Minn. 1962)
Vol I: Benedictine authors; II: Benedictine subjects. Includes locations of works in American Benedictine houses.

9

Bauerreiss, Romuald 'Bibliographie der benediktinischen Zeitschriften und Sammelwerke' and 'Bibliographie der benediktinischen Zeitschriften und Schriftenreihen II (1949)' *Stud Mitt* 46 (1928) 118-21, 397-8 and 62 (1949-50) 48-55
Cf Kapsner 8, I, 647-64, nos 13126-13428.

10

Albareda, Anselm M. *Bibliografía de la regla benedictina* (Montserrat 1933)
With introduction on the text, versions, and influence. For later works, see Romuald Bauerreiss in *Stud Mitt* 58 (1940) 3-20; Cousin **51**, 150-4; and de Vogüé **742**.

11

Jaspert, Bernd 'Regula Magistri – Regula Benedicti. Bibliographie ihrer historisch-kritischen Erforschung 1938-1970' *Stud mon* 13 (1971) 129-71 563 items. Supplants bibliography by Odo Zimmermann in *American Benedictine Review* 10 (1959) 86-106.

12

Ziegelbauer, Magnoald *Historia rei literariae ordinis S Benedicti* 4 vols (Augsburg - Würzburg 1754).

13

Martin, Jean-Baptiste 'Bibliographie liturgique de l'ordre de Saint Benoît' *Rev Mab* 11 (1921) 47-59, 125-49; 12 (1922) 181-8; 13 (1923) 188-97; 14 (1924) 96-107 321 items.

Cistercians

14

Donkin, Robert A. *A Check List of Printed Works Relating to the Cistercian Order as a Whole and to the Houses of the British Isles in Particular* (Documentation cistercienne 2; Rochefort 1969).

15

Janauschek, Leopold *Bibliographia bernardina* (Xenia bernardina 4; Vienna 1891).

16

Bouton, Jean de la Croix *Bibliographie bernardine 1891-1957* (Commission d'histoire de l'ordre de Cîteaux 5; Paris 1958).

17

Manning, Eugène *Bibliographie bernardine 1957-1970* (Documentation cistercienne 6; Rochefort 1972).

SERIAL

18

Revue d'histoire ecclésiastique: Bibliographie (Louvain 1900ff)
This massive classified bibliography covers the whole range of church history. Secondary works on monasticism are mostly listed under 'Histoire de l'ascétisme' (III, 3, D) and 'Histoire des corporations religieuses' (III, 4).

19
Bulletin d'histoire bénédictine (Maredsous 1907ff)
Supplement to the *Rev bén* (see **26**). Seven volumes have appeared, of
which the last covers 1964-9. It now concentrates almost exclusively on
the Benedictine order, but the early volumes also cover pre- and non-
Benedictine monasticism.

20
Bulletin d'histoire monastique (Ligugé 1936-66)
Supplement to the *Rev Mab* (see **27**). Three volumes have appeared covering 1936-43, 1944-58, and 1959-66. The earlier *Chronique bibliographique*
formed part of the *Rev Mab* until 1926 and then appeared as two separately-
paginated volumes covering 1927-30 and 1931-5. There is an index to the
entire series in the *Tables générales* of the *Rev Mab*, vols 1-57, published
hors-série, nos 233-9 (1968-70). Varies in scope, but concentrates on France.

21
Bauerreiss, Romuald 'Bibliographia benedictina 1937,' 'Bibliographia
benedictina 1938,' and 'Bibliographia benedictina 1939-52' *Stud Mitt* 56
(1938) [1]-[14], 57 (1939) [15]-[28], 64 (1952) [29]-[153]
Forms a continuously-paginated volume, with index, covering 1937-52.

22
Bulletin de spiritualité monastique (Scourmont 1959ff)
Supplement to *Coll cist* (see **30**). One volume a year appeared until 1966;
vol 8 covers 1967-70. *Tables générales* published as supplement to *Coll cist*
32 (1970).

23
Rouse, Richard H. *Serial Bibliographies for Medieval Studies* (Publications
of the Center for Medieval and Renaissance Studies 3; Berkeley - Los
Angeles 1969)
Pp 73-6, nos 147-55, cover monasticism.

Journals

GENERAL

24

Studia monastica (Montserrat 1959ff).

BENEDICTINE

25

Studien und Mitteilungen zur Geschichte des Benediktiner-ordens und seiner Zweige (Brünn/Würzburg - Vienna/Salzburg/Munich/[since 1967] Ottobeuren 1880ff)
The title has varied over the years. Only the more important changes are mentioned here: Vols 1-2: *Wissenschaftliche Studien und Mittheilungen aus dem Benedictiner-Orden mit besonderer Berücksichtigung der Ordensgeschichte und Statistik*; 3: the same without *Wissenschaftliche*; 4-31: *Studien und Mittheilungen aus dem Benedictiner- und dem Cistercienser-Orden mit besonderer Berücksichtigung der Ordensgeschichte und Statistik*. There is a general index to vols 1-50 (1880-1932) in 56 (1938) 1-75.

26

Revue bénédictine (Maredsous 1884ff)
Vols 1-2: *Le messager des fidèles. Petite revue bénédictine*; 3-6: *Le messager des fidèles. Revue bénédictine*. Three volumes of general indices published in 1905, 1945, and 1971.

27

Revue Mabillon (Paris - Ligugé/Ligugé 1905ff)
Cf **20** for indices.

28
Benedictina (Rome 1947ff).

CISTERCIAN

29
Cistercienser-Chronik (Bregenz 1889ff).

30
Collectanea cisterciensia (Rome - Westmalle/Westmalle/Scourmont 1934ff)
Vols 1-26: *Collectanea ordinis Cisterciensium reformatorum.*

31
Analecta cisterciensia (Rome 1945ff)
Vols 1-20: *Analecta sacri ordinis cisterciensis.*

32
Cîteaux (Westmalle/Achel 1950ff)
Vols 1-9: *Cîteaux in de Nederlanden.*

PREMONSTRATENSIAN

33
Analecta praemonstratensia (Tongerloo/Averbode 1925ff).

Series

34
Kirchenrechtliche Abhandlungen (Stuttgart 1902ff).

35
Archives de la France monastique (Paris - Ligugé 1905ff).

36
Beiträge zur Geschichte des alten Mönchtums und des Benediktinerordens
(Münster W. 1912ff).

37
Studia Anselmiana (Rome 1933ff).

Dictionaries

38
*A Dictionary of Christian Biography, Literature, Sects and Doctrines
[during the First Eight Centuries]* ed William Smith and Henry Wace
4 vols (London 1877-87).

39
Dictionnaire d'archéologie chrétienne et de liturgie ed Fernand Cabrol and
Henri Leclercq. 15 vols in 30 (Paris 1907-53).

40
Dictionnaire d'histoire et de géographie ecclésiastiques ed Alfred
Baudrillart et al. 18 vols in 102 fascs to date (Paris 1912ff).

41
Dictionnaire de spiritualité, ascétique et mystique, doctrine et histoire ed
Marcel Viller et al. 8 vols in 56 fascs to date (Paris 1932ff).

42
The Oxford Dictionary of the Christian Church (1957) 2nd ed Frank L.
Cross and Elizabeth A. Livingstone (Oxford 1974).

Atlases

Cf regional maps (354-6, 503) and other local works.

43
Poole, Reginald Lane *Historical Atlas of Modern Europe from the Decline of the Roman Empire* (Oxford 1902)
Maps of monastic interest include 19 (England), 26 (Scotland), 30 (Ireland), 37 (Germany), 57 (France), 61 (Spain), and 69 (Italy).

44
Jedin, Hubert, Kenneth Scott Latourette, and Jochen Martin *Atlas zur Kirchengeschichte. Die christlichen Kirchen in Geschichte und Gegenwart* (Freiburg B. - Basel - Vienna, etc 1970)
Maps of monastic interest include 11 (Egypt), 12 (North Syria), 14 (early West), 25 (Irish and Anglo-Saxon missions), 37 (Francia, Bavaria, North Italy to 768), 38 (Jacobite), 39 (Byzantine), 45 (Basilian in South Italy and Sicily), 47 (Cluny), 48 (neo-Cluniac in Germany), 49 (Camaldoli, Vallombrosa), 50 (regular canons to 1250), 51 (Carthusians), 52-3 (Cistercians), 54 (Premonstratensians), 67 (Bursfeld, Kastl, Melk), and 68 (Windesheim and Brethren of Common Life).

45
Van der Meer, Frédéric [Frederik] *Atlas de l'ordre cistercien* (Amsterdam - Brussels 1965)
See the revisions and corrections by Maur Cocheril in *Cîteaux* 17 (1966) 119-44; Edgar Krausen and Polykarp Zakar in *Anal cist* 22 (1966) 279-90; Felix Vongrey and Ferenc Hervay in *Anal cist* 23 (1967) 115-52; Franz Schrader in *Cîteaux* 21 (1970) 265-78.

MEDIEVAL MONASTICISM

PART II: MONASTIC HISTORY

General

COLLECTIVE WORKS

46
Cambridge Medieval History ed Henry M. Gwatkin et al. 8 vols and vol of
maps (Cambridge 1911-36). 2nd ed of I (1924) and of IV, in 2 vols (1967)
See especially the chapters by Edward Cuthbert Butler on early monasticism
(I) and by Alexander Hamilton Thompson on monastic orders (V).

47
Histoire de l'église ed Augustin Fliche and Victor Martin. 21 vols in 24 to
date (Paris 1934ff)
See **272, 585**, and the chapters by Pierre de Labriolle on early monasticism
(III), René Aigrain on early western monasticism (V), and by Auguste
Dumas on monasticism in ninth to eleventh centuries (VII).

GENERAL SURVEYS

48
Harnack, Adolf [von] *Das Möncht[h]um, seine Ideale und seine Geschichte.*
Eine kirchenhistorische Vorlesung (Giessen 1881; Eng trans by E. E.
Kellett 1901)
Later 'editions' are reprints.

49
Berlière, Ursmer *L'ordre monastique des origines au XIIᵉ siècle* (1912)
3rd ed (Collection pax 1; Lille - Paris - Maredsous 1924)
Brief survey down to twelfth century, with bibliographies.

50
Workman, Herbert B. *The Evolution of the Monastic Ideal from the Earliest Times down to the Coming of the Friars* (London 1913; repr with intro by David Knowles 1962).

51
Cousin, Patrice *Précis d'histoire monastique* ([Paris] [1956])
Longer survey of all monastic history, with full (but often unreliable) bibliographies.

52
Knowles, David *Christian Monasticism* (London 1969)
Brief survey of all monastic history.

MONASTIC HISTORIOGRAPHY

Cf 944.

53
Hilpisch, Stephanus 'St Benedikt in der neueren Hagiographie' *Stud Mitt* 61 (1947-8) 114-25; and 'Benediktinerhistoriker der neueren Zeit' *Beten und Arbeiten aus Geschichte und Gegenwart benediktinischen Lebens* ed Theodor Bogler (Liturgie und Mönchtum 28; Maria Laach 1961) 15-23.

54
Penco, Gregorio 'Dove va la storiografia monastica italiana?' *Stud mon* 13 (1971) 405-29; and 'Erudizione e storiografia monastica in Italia nei primi decenni del novecento' *Benedictina* 19 (1972) 1-16
On Alfredo Schuster, Placido Lugano, et al.

55
Constable, Giles 'The Study of Monastic History Today' *Essays on the Reconstruction of Medieval History* ed Vaclav Mudroch and G. S. Couse (Montreal - London 1974) 21-51.

SOCIOLOGY OF MONASTICISM

56
Moulin, Léo 'Pour une sociologie des ordres religieux' *Social Compass* 10 (1963) 145-70; and *Le monde vivant des religieux. Dominicains, Jésuites, Bénédictins...* (Paris 1964)
Mostly contemporary.

57
Séguy, Jean 'Une sociologie des sociétés imaginées: monachisme et utopie'
Annales 26 (1971) 328-54.

Benedictine

Cf 579-82.

58
Blazovich, Augustin *Soziologie des Mönchtums und der Benediktinerregel*
(Vienna 1954).

59
Brechter, Heinrich Suso 'Die soziologische Gestalt des Benediktinertums
in seinen Anfängen' *Benedictus. Der Vater der Abendlandes 547-1947.
Weihegabe der Erzabtei St Ottilien zum vierzehnhundertsten Todesjahr* ed
Heinrich Suso Brechter (Munich 1947) 57-76.

Byzantine

60
Savramis [Sabramēs], Demosthenes *Zur Soziologie des byzantinischen
Mönchtums* (Leiden - Cologne 1962).

Eastern Monasticism

Cf 739-40, 854, 891, 944, 983-5, 1007, 1012-13, 1015-16, 1019-21, 1024, 1027, 1030.

GENERAL

61
Besse, Jean-Martial *Les moines d'Orient antérieurs au concile de Chalcédoine (451)* (Paris - Poitiers 1900).

62
Il monachesimo orientale. Atti del convegno di studi orientali che sul predetto tema si tenne a Roma, sotto la direzione del Pontificio Istituto orientale, nei giorni 9, 10, 11 e 12 aprile 1958 (Orientalia christiana analecta 153; Rome 1958)
See **105**.

ORIGINS

63
Berlière, Ursmer 'Les origines du monachisme et la critique moderne'
Rev bén 8 (1891) 1-19, 49-69.

64
Schiwietz [Siwiec], Stephan *Das morgenländische Mönchtum* 3 vols
(Mainz/Mödhling bei Wien 1904-38)
Vol I (1904): Asceticism of the first three centuries and Egyptian monasticism in the fourth century; II (1913): Sinai and Palestine in the fourth century; III (1938): Syria, Mesopotamia, and Persia in the fourth and fifth centuries.

65

Gobillot, Philippe 'Les origines du monachisme chrétien et l'ancienne
religion de l'Egypt' *Recherches de science religieuse* 10 (1920) 303-54;
11 (1921) 29-86, 168-213, 328-61; 12 (1922) 46-68.

66

Heussi, Karl *Der Ursprung des Mönchtums* (Tübingen 1936)
Cf Louis Théophile Lefort in *Rev d'hist ecc* 33 (1937) 341-8.

67

Lietzmann, Hans *Geschichte der alten Kirche, IV: Die Zeit der Kirchen-
väter* (Berlin 1944; Eng trans by Bertram L. Wolff 1951)
Pp 116-92 on monasticism.

68

Vööbus, Arthur *History of Asceticism in the Syrian Orient: A Contribution
to the History of Culture in the Near East* 2 vols (Corpus scriptorum
christianorum orientalium 184, 197 [= Subsidia 14, 17]; Louvain 1958-60)
Vol I: The origin of asceticism. Early monasticism in Persia; II: Early
monasticism in Mesopotamia and Syria.

69

Pericoli Ridolfini, Francesco S. *Alle origini del monachesimo. Le
convergenze esseniche* (Rome 1966)
Compares Hellenistic and Essene religious life and theory with fourth- and
fifth-century monasticism.

70

Chitty, Derwas J. *The Desert a City: An Introduction to the Study of
Egyptian and Palestinian Monasticism under the Christian Empire*
(Oxford 1966).

EASTERN SAINTS

71

Delehaye, Hippolyte *Les saints stylites* (Subsidia hagiographica 14;
Brussels - Paris 1923).

72

Draguet, René *Les pères du désert* (Paris 1949)
Translations with introduction on pp v-lx.

73

Festugière, André-Jean *Les moines d'Orient* 4 vols in 7 parts (Paris

1961-5)
Vol I: Introduction to Eastern monasticism; II-IV: Translations of lives of saints from Constantinople, Palestine, and Egypt.

74
Halkin, François *Saints moines d'Orient* (Variorum Reprints Collected Studies 17; London 1973)
Not seen.

MONKS AND SOCIETY

75
Dodds, Eric R. *Pagan and Christian in an Age of Anxiety: Some Aspects of Religious Experience from Marcus Aurelius to Constantine* (Wiles Lectures 1963; Cambridge 1965).

76
Frend, William H. C. 'The Monks and the Survival of the East Roman Empire in the Fifth Century' *Past and Present* 54 (1972) 3-24.

77
Bacht, Heinrich 'Die Rolle des orientalischen Mönchtums in den kirchen-politischen Auseinandersetzungen um Chalkedon (431-519)' *Das Konzil von Chalkedon. Geschichte und Gegenwart* (Würzburg 1953) II, 193-314
Cf also the article by Leo Ueding (II, 569-676) on the significance for monasticism of the canons of the Council of Chalcedon.

BYZANTINE MONASTICISM

Cf **60, 144, 199, 348, 525-32, 639-41, 668-71, 790, 797, 809, 960-4.**

78
Holl, Karl 'Ueber das griechische Mönchtum' *Preussische Jahrbücher* 94 (1898) 407-24; repr in his *Gesammelte Aufsätze zur Kirchengeschichte*, II: *Der Osten* (Tübingen 1928) 270-82.

79
Granić, Branco 'Die rechtliche Stellung und Organisation der griechischen Klöster nach dem justinianischen Recht' *Byzantinische Zs* 29 (1929) 6-34; and 'Das Klosterwesen in der Novellengesetzgebung Kaiser Leons des Weisen' *ibid* 31 (1931) 61-9.

80

Meester, Placide de *De monachico statu juxta disciplinam byzantinam* (Sacra congregazione per la chiesa orientale: Codificazione canonica orientale: Fonti, 2 S, 10; Vatican City 1942).

81

Janin, Raymond 'Le monachisme byzantin au moyen âge. Commende et typica (X^e-XIVe siècle)' *Revue des études byzantines* 22 (1964) 5-44.

82

Hussey, Joan M. 'Byzantine Monasticism' *Cambridge Medieval History* **46**, IV.2, 161-84 and (bibliography) 439-43.

83

Charanis, Peter 'The Monk as an Element of Byzantine Society' *Dumbarton Oaks Papers* 25 (1971) 63-84.

EGYPT

Cf 6.

84

Mackean, William H. *Christian Monasticism in Egypt to the Close of the Fourth Century* (London 1920).

85

Bousset, Wilhelm *Apophthegmata. Studien zur Geschichte des ältesten Mönchtums* (Tübingen 1923).

86

Bousset, Wilhelm 'Das Mönchtum der sketischen Wüste' *Zs für KG* 42 (1923) 1-41.

87

Evelyn-White, Hugh G. *The Monasteries of the Wâdi 'n Natrûn* 3 vols [II-III ed Walter Hauser] (New York 1926-33)
Vol I: New Coptic texts from the Monastery of St Macarius; II: History of the monasteries of Nitria and Scetis; III: Architecture and archaeology.

88

Cauwenbergh, Paul van *Etude sur les moines d'Egypte depuis le concile de Chalcédoine (451) jusqu'à l'invasion arabe (640)* (Louvain - Paris 1914).

89

Barison, Paola 'Ricerche sui monasteri dell'Egitto bizantino ed arabo secondo i documenti dei papiri greci' *Aegyptus* 18 (1938) 29-148

Covers fourth to eighth centuries, with sections on organization and administration (pp 32-65) and a list of monasteries (pp 66-148).

Anthony

90
Reitzenstein, Richard *Des Athanasius Werk über das Leben des Antonius. Ein philologischer Beitrag zur Geschichte des Mönchtums* (Sitzungsberichte der Heidelberger Akademie der Wissenschaften. Philosophisch-historische Klasse 1914.8; Heidelberg 1914).

91
Dörries, Hermann 'Die Vita Antonii als Geschichtsquelle' *Nachrichten der Akademie der Wissenschaften in Göttingen. Philologisch-historische Klasse* 1949 (no 14) 359-410 and *Wort und Stunde* 132, I, 145-224.

92
Antonius Magnus Eremita 356-1956. Studia ad antiquum monachismum spectantia ed Basilius Steidle (Stud Ans 38; Rome 1956)
See **95, 979**. Cf also the introduction by Christine Mohrmann to the new edition of the *Vita Antonii* by Gerhardus J. M. Bartelink (Milan 1974) [not seen].

Pachomius

Cf **836, 944**.

93
Ladeuze, Paulin *Etude sur le cénobitisme pakhomien pendant le IVe siècle et la première moitié du Ve* (Louvain - Paris 1898).

94
Lehmann, Konstantin 'Die Entstehung der Freiheitsstrafe in den Klöstern des heiligen Pachomius' *Sav-Zs, Kan Abt* 37 (1951) 1-94.

95
Bacht, Heinrich 'Antonius und Pachomius. Von der Anachorese zum Cönobitentum' *Antonius Magnus* 92, 66-107.

96
Ruppert, Fidelis *Das pachomianische Mönchtum und die Anfänge klösterlichen Gehorsams* (Münsterschwarzacher Studien 20; Münsterschwarzach 1971).

Cassian

Cf **847, 944.**

97
Chadwick, Owen *John Cassian* (1950) 2nd ed (Cambridge 1968).

98
Weber, Hans-Oskar *Die Stellung des Johannes Cassianus zur ausserpacho-mianischen Mönchstradition. Eine Quellenuntersuchung* (Beiträge 24; Münster W. 1961).

99
Guy, Jean-Claude *Jean Cassien. Vie et doctrine spirituelle* (Collection théologie, pastorale et spiritualité: Recherches et synthèses 9; Paris 1961) Selected texts with introduction on pp 11-62.

100
Leroy, Julien 'Le cénobitisme chez Cassien' *Revue d'ascétique et de mystique* 43 (1967) 121-58.

Palladius and the *Lausiac History*

101
Reitzenstein, Richard. Historia monachorum *und* Historia lausiaca. *Eine Studie zur Geschichte des Mönchtums und der frühchristlichen Begriffe Gnostiker und Pneumatiker* (Forschungen zur Religion und Literatur des Alten und Neuen Testaments 24 [NS, 7]; Göttingen 1916).

102
Draguet, René 'L'*Histoire lausiaque*. Une oeuvre écrite dans l'esprit d'Evagre' *Rev d'hist ecc* 41 (1946) 321-64; 42 (1947) 5-49
A technical comparison with brief conclusion. Cf also Draguet's criticism of Edward Cuthbert Butler's edition of the *Lausiac History* in *Muséon* 63 (1950) 205-30 and 68 (1955) 239-58, and Derwas Chitty's defense of Butler in *Journal of Theological Studies* NS, 6 (1955) 102-10.

PALESTINE

103
Gordini, Gian Domenico 'Il monachesimo romano in Palestina nel IV secolo' *St Martin* **415,** 85-107.

104
Genier, Raymond *Vie de Saint Euthyme le Grand (377-473).* *Les moines et l'église en Palestine au* V^e *siècle* (Paris 1909).

105
Corbo, Virgilio 'L'ambiente materiale della vita dei monaci di Palestina nel periodo bizantino' *Monachesimo orientale* **62**, 235-57.

LEBANON

106
Mahfoud, Georges-Joseph *L'organisation monastique dans l'église maronite. Etude historique* (Bibliothèque de l'Université Saint-Esprit: Kaslik - Jounieh - Liban 1; Beirut 1967) Pp 73-128 on origins and history of Maronite monasticism from the tenth to the seventeenth century.

SYRIA

Cf **335, 944**.

107
Jargy, Simon 'Les origines du monachisme en Syrie et en Mésopotamie' *Proche-Orient chrétien* 2 (1952) 110-24; and 'Les premiers instituts monastiques et les principaux représentants du monachisme syrien au IVe siècle' *ibid* 4 (1954) 106-17.

108
Hendriks, Olaf 'L'activité apostolique des premiers moines syriens' *Proche-Orient chrétien* 8 (1958) 3-25; and 'La vie quotidienne du moine syrien oriental [primitif]' *L'Orient syrien* 5 (1960) 293-330, 401-31.

109
Gribomont, Jean 'Le monachisme au sein de l'église en Syrie et en Cappadoce' *Stud mon* 7 (1965) 7-24.

110
Baker, Aelred 'Syriac and the Origins of Monasticism' *Downside Review* 86 (1968) 342-53.

OUTSIDE THE ROMAN EMPIRE

111
Labourt, Jérôme *Le christianisme dans l'empire perse sous la dynastie sassanide (224-632)* (Paris 1904)
Argues that monasticism in Persia was independent from Egypt.

112
Vööbus, Arthur 'The Origin of Monasticism in Mesopotamia' *Church History* 20.4 (1951) 27-37
Cf **68**.

113
Fiey, Jean Maurice *Assyrie chrétienne. Contribution à l'étude de l'histoire et de la géographie ecclésiastiques et monastiques du nord de l'Iraq* 3 vols [I-II paged consecutively] (Recherches publiées sous la direction de l'Institut de lettres orientales de Beyrouth 22-23, 42; Beirut 1965-8).

ASIA MINOR

114
Gribomont, Jean 'Le monachisme au IVe s. en Asie Mineure: de Ganges au Messalianisme' *Studia patristica: Papers Presented to the Second International Conference on Patristic Studies Held at Christ Church, Oxford, 1955* ed Kurt Aland and Frank L. Cross, II (Texte und Untersuchungen zur Geschichte der altchristlichen Literatur 64 [5 S, 9]; Berlin 1957) 400-15.

Basil

Cf **738, 740, 944, 992**.

115
Clarke, William K. Lowther *St Basil the Great: A Study in Monasticism* (Cambridge 1913)
Cf also his introduction to *The Ascetic Works of S Basil* (London 1925).

116
Amand, David [= Emmanuel Amand de Mendieta] *L'ascèse monastique de Saint Basile. Essai historique* (Maredsous 1949).

117
Amand de Mendieta, Emmanuel 'Le système cénobitique basilien comparé au système cénobitique pachômien' *Revue de l'histoire des religions* 152 (1957) 31-80.

Constantinople

118
Marin, Eugène *Les moines de Constantinople depuis la fondation de la ville jusqu'à la mort de Photius (330-898)* (Paris 1897)
Cf Jules Pargoire in *Revue des questions historiques* 65 (1899) 67-143, criticising some of Marin's views.

119
Dagron, Gilbert 'Les moines et la ville. Le monachisme à Constantinople jusqu'au concile de Chalcédoine (451)' *Centre de recherche d'histoire et civilisation byzantines: Travaux et mémoires* 4 (1970) 229-76.

120
Leroy, Julien *Studitisches Mönchtum. Spiritualität und Lebensform* trans Mirjam Prager (Geist und Leben der Ostkirche 4; Graz - Vienna - Cologne 1969)
Translated from the manuscript. Cf **963**.

GREECE

121
Amand de Mendieta, Emmanuel *La presqu'île des Caloyers. Le Mont-Athos* (Bruges 1955; Eng trans by Michael R. Bruce 1972)
Pp 9-44 on the tenth to fifteenth centuries.

122
Le millénaire du Mont Athos, 963-1963. Etudes et mélanges 2 vols (I: Chevetogne 1963; II: Actes du 'Convegno internazionale di studio' à la Fondazione Giorgio Cini [3-6 septembre 1963] à Venise, Venice - Chevetogne 1964)
See **199, 303**; includes bibliography on Mt Athos (II, 337-495).

123
Nicol, Donald M. *Meteora: The Rock Monasteries of Thessaly* (London 1963).

RUSSIA

Cf 965.

124

Rouët de Journel, Marie-Joseph *Monachisme et monastères russes* (Paris 1952)
Includes sections on historical development and on individual monasteries.

125

Smolitsch, Igor *Russisches Mönchtum. Entstehung, Entwicklung und Wesen 988-1917* (Das östliche Christentum, NS, 10-11; Würzburg 1953)
Pp 50-118 on the Middle Ages.

126

Casey, Robert P. 'Early Russian Monasticism' *Orientalia christiana periodica* 19 (1953) 372-423.

127

Dvornik, Francis 'Les bénédictins et la christianisation de la Russie' *L'église et les églises. 1054-1954. Etudes et travaux sur l'unité chrétienne offerts à Dom Lambert Beauduin* (Collection Irénikon; Chevetogne 1954-55) I, 323-49; revised trans in *Benediktinische Monatschrift (Erbe und Auftrag)* 35 (1959) 292-310.

Western Monasticism: Chronological

GENERAL

Short Surveys

128

Southern, Richard W. *Western Society and the Church in the Middle Ages* (Pelican History of the Church 2; Harmondsworth 1970) Pp 214-99 on religious orders.

129

Pacaut, Marcel *Les ordres monastiques et religieux au moyen âge* (Paris 1970).

Collected Articles by Individual Authors

Cf **74, 78, 207, 213, 259, 301, 344, 365-6, 374, 485-7, 523-4, 636, 689, 813, 825, 939, 946, 962, 996-8, 1026.**

130

Berlière, Ursmer *Mélanges d'histoire bénédictine* 4 vols (Maredsous 1897-1902)

See **587**.

131

Cilento, Vincenzo *Medio evo monastico e scolastico* (Milan - Naples 1961).

132

Dörries, Hermann *Wort und Stunde* 3 vols (Göttingen 1966-70)

See **91, 285, 1007, 1030.**

133

Gasquet, Francis Aidan *Monastic Life in the Middle Ages* (London 1922)
See **583**. On Gasquet as an historian, see Knowles **136**, 240-63.

134

Hirsch, Hans *Aufsätze zur mittelalterlichen Urkundenforschung* ed
Theodor Mayer (Darmstadt 1965).

135

Knowles, David *Great Historical Enterprises. Problems in Monastic History*
(London - Edinburgh 1963)
Includes articles on the Bollandists and Maurists, the *Regula Magistri* and
Rule of St Benedict, and early Cistercian documents (**251**).

136

Knowles, David *The Historian and Character and Other Essays*
(Cambridge 1963)
See **147, 149**. Includes bibliography of Knowles's works (pp 363-73).

137

Schreiber, Georg *Gemeinschaften des Mittelalters. Recht und Verfassung.*
Kult und Frömmigkeit (Gesammelte Abhandlungen 1; Münster W. 1948)
See **722, 866**.

138

Williams, Watkin *Monastic Studies* (Publications of the University of
Manchester 262: Historical Series 76; Manchester 1938)
Articles on Cluny, Cîteaux, Benedict of Aniane, Bernard, Peter the
Venerable, et al.

Orders and Congregations

Cf **244, 378-9, 499-501, 583-9**.

139

[Hélyot, Pierre and Maximilien Bullot] *Histoire des ordres monastiques,*
religieux et militaires et des congrégations séculières de l'un et de l'autre
sexe 8 vols (Paris 1714-19; and later reprints).

140

Heimbucher, Max *Die Orden und Kongregationen der katholischen Kirche*
(1896-7) 3rd ed 2 vols (Paderborn 1933-4).

141

Ordini e congregazioni religiose ed Mario Escobar. 2 vols (Turin 1951-3)

Mostly modern, but with chapters on the Benedictines (Tommaso Leccisotti), Cistercians (Vincent Hermans), Premonstratensians (Cyriel Nys), and Augustinian Canons (Carlo Egger).

142
Molitor, Raphael *Aus der Rechtsgeschichte benediktinischer Verbände. Untersuchungen und Skizzen* 3 vols (Münster W. 1928-33)
Cf Paul Volk in *Rev bén* 42 (1930) 171-6 and, on Molitor and his work, Gerhard Oesterle in *Stud Mitt* 73 (1962) 14-40.

143
Dammertz, Viktor *Das Verfassungsrecht der benediktinischen Mönchskongregationen in Geschichte und Gegenwart* (Kirchengeschichtliche Quellen und Studien 6; St Ottilien 1963)
Mostly contemporary but with some historical material.

144
Schreiber, Georg 'Religiöse Verbände in mittelalterlicher Wertung. Lateinischer Westen und griechischer Osten' *Historisches Jahrbuch* 62-69 (1949) 284-358
Studies the views on orders of Anselm of Havelberg and James of Vitry. Cf also his articles in **137**.

145
Dubois, Jacques 'Les ordres religieux au XIIe siècle selon la curie romaine' *Rev bén* 78 (1968) 283-309.

Benedictine Monasticism

Cf **8-13, 53, 59, 141-3**.

146
Yepes, Antonio de *Coronica general de la orden de San Benito* 7 vols (Irache 1609-21)
Especially important for Spain. Comes down to 1169. Cf on this work the introduction by Justo Pérez de Urbel in vol I of the partial reprint (Madrid 1959-60).

147
Mabillon, Jean *Annales ordinis Sancti Benedicti* 6 vols (Paris 1703-39)
According to Coulton **271**, I, xxvi 'This ... forms the most valuable contribution, beyond all comparison, ever made to monastic history.' On Mabillon, cf Knowles **136**, 213-39.

148

Montalembert, Charles [Forbes René de Tryon, comte] de *Les moines d'Occident depuis Saint Benoît jusqu'à Saint Bernard* 7 vols (Paris 1860-77; Eng trans 1861-79 and again, with an intro by Francis Aidan Gasquet [583], 1896)
An influential work, largely based on Mabillon **147**. Cf also the first version, published posthumously under the title *Précis d'histoire monastique des origines à la fin du XIe siècle* (Paris 1934).

149

Butler, Edward Cuthbert *Benedictine Monachism. Studies in Benedictine Life and Rule* (1919) 2nd ed (London 1924; repr with intro by David Knowles 1962)
On Butler and his work, see Knowles **136**, 264-362.

150

Hilpisch, Stephanus *Geschichte des benediktinischen Mönchtums in ihren Grundzügen dargestellt* (Freiburg B. 1929; Eng trans by Justus Wirth 1936 [not seen])
General survey down to modern times.

151

Knowles, David *The Benedictines* (London 1929; repr with intro by J. Hugh Diman 1930).

152

Pérez de Urbel, Justo *Historia de la orden benedictina* (Madrid 1941)
General survey down to modern times.

153

Schmitz, Philibert *Histoire de l'ordre de Saint-Benoît* 7 vols 2nd ed of I-II (Maredsous 1948-56)
The most extensive modern general survey, coming down to modern times, with bibliographies; vol VII deals with nuns. On Schmitz and his work, see Tomás Moral in *American Benedictine Review* 15 (1964) 458-65.

154

Hilpisch, Stephanus *Das Benediktinertum im Wandel der Zeiten* (Benediktinisches Geistesleben 2; St Ottilien 1950; Eng trans by Leonard J. Doyle 1958).

155

Daly, Lowrie *Benedictine Monasticism: Its Formation and Development through the 12th Century* (New York 1965).

Collective Works

156
Studia benedictina in memoriam gloriosi ante saecula XIV transitus S P Benedicti (Stud Ans 18-19; Rome 1947)
See **604, 764**.

157
Mélanges bénédictins publiés à l'occasion du XIVe centenaire de la mort de Saint Benoît par les moines de l'abbaye de Saint-Jérôme de Rome (Abbaye S Wandrille 1947)
See **171, 189, 816**.

158
Commentationes in regulam S Benedicti ed Basilius Steidle (Stud Ans 42; Rome 1957)
See **176**.

Benedictine Saints

159
Zimmermann, Alfons M. *Kalendarium benedictinum. Die Heiligen und Seligen des Benediktinerordens und seiner Zweige* 4 vols (Metten 1933-8).

FOURTH TO TENTH CENTURIES

General

160
Lorenz, Rudolf 'Die Anfänge des abendländischen Mönchtums im 4. Jahrhundert' *Zs für KG* 77 (1966) 1-61.

161
Il monachesimo nell'alto medioevo e la formazione della civiltà occidentale (Settimane di studio del Centro italiano di studi sull'alto medioevo 4; Spoleto 1957)
See **190, 218, 405, 418, 422, 490, 509, 880**.

162
Décarreaux, Jean *Les moines et la civilisation en Occident. Des invasions à Charlemagne* (Signes des temps 13; [Paris] [1962]; Eng trans by Charlotte Haldane 1964).

163

Prinz, Friedrich *Frühes Mönchtum im Frankenreich. Kultur und Gesellschaft in Gallien, den Rheinlanden und Bayern am Beispiel der monastischen Entwicklung (4. bis 8. Jahrhundert)* (Munich - Vienna 1965)
With annex of maps.

164

Sullivan, Richard E. 'Some Influences of Monasticism on Fourth and Fifth Century Society' *Studies in Medieval Culture* 2 (1966) 19-34.

165

McLaughlin, Terence P. *Le très ancien droit monastique de l'occident. Etude sur le développement général du monachisme et ses rapports avec l'église seculière et le monde laïque de Saint Benoît de Nursie à Saint Benoît d'Aniane* (Archives 38; Ligugé - Paris 1935).

166

Levison, Wilhelm *England and the Continent in the Eighth Century* (Ford Lectures 1943; Oxford 1946)
Includes sections on monastic culture, privileges, and missions.

167

Schroll, Mary Alfred *Benedictine Monasticism as Reflected in the Warnefrid-Hildemar Commentaries on the Rule* (New York 1941)
Chapters on monastic organization, economy, discipline, and life in the eighth and ninth centuries.

North Africa

168

Folliet, Georges 'Aux origines de l'ascétisme et du cénobitisme africain' *St Martin* **415**, 25-44.

169

Gavigan, John Joseph *De vita monastica in Africa septentrionali inde a temporibus S Augustini usque ad invasiones Arabum* (Bibliotheca augustiniana medii aevi 2 S, 1; Turin 1962).

The Fathers of the Church

Ambrose

Cf **1022**.

170
Roberti, Arnaldo 'S Ambrogio e il monachismo' *La scuola cattolica* 68 (1940) 140-59, 236-53.

Jerome

Cf 878, 1022.

171
Antin, Paul *Essai sur Saint Jérôme* (Paris 1951)
Pp 109-45 on his monastic life and teaching. See also Antin's articles in **157** (reprinted in his *Recueil sur Saint Jérôme* [Latomus 95; Brussels 1968], pp 101-33) and **944**.

172
Coleiro, E. 'Monasticism in St Jerome's Letters and Lives of the Hermits' *Melita Theologica* 4 (1951) 1-13, 61-74; 5 (1952) 17-30.

Augustine

Cf 169, 738, 757, 944, 953, 1022.

173
Zumkeller, Adolar *Das Mönchtum des heiligen Augustinus* (1950) 2nd ed (Cassiciacum 11; Würzburg 1968).

174
Cilleruelo, Lope *El monacato de San Agustín* (Archivo teológico agustiniano 6; Valladolid 1966).

Gregory the Great

Cf 944, 953.

175
Porcel, Olegario M. *La doctrina monastica de San Gregorio Magno y la 'Regula monachorum'* (Madrid 1950)
Cf also his article in *Monastica* I (Scripta et documenta 12; Montserrat 1960) 1-95, dealing with Gregory's views on the abbot, admission, 'conversatio', etc.

176
Hallinger, Kassius 'Papst Gregor der Grosse und der hl Benedikt'
Commentationes **158**, 231-319
Cf Gregorio Penco *ibid* 321-45.

Monastic Missionaries

Cf **398-406**.

Columbanus

177
Mélanges colombaniens. Actes du Congrès international de Luxeuil 20-23 juillet 1950 (Bibliothèque de la Société d'histoire ecclésiastique de la France; Luxeuil - Paris [1951]).
178
San Colombano e la sua opera in Italia. Convegno storico colombaniano. Bobbio 1-2 settembre 1951 (Bobbio 1953).

Pirmin

179
Jecker, Gall *Die Heimat des hl Pirmin des Apostels der Alamannen* (Beiträge 13; Münster W. 1927)
Argues Pirmin came from southern France.
180
Angenendt, Arnold E. *Monachi peregrini. Studien zu Pirmin und den monastischen Vorstellungen des frühen Mittelalters* (Münstersche Mittelalter-Schriften 6; Munich 1972)
Argues against Jecker **179** that Pirmin reflected Iro-Frankish usage.

Boniface

181
Lortz, Josef 'Untersuchungen zur Missionsmethode und zur Frömmigkeit des hl Bonifatius nach seinen Briefen' *Willibrordus* ed Nikolaus Goetzinger (Luxemburg 1940) 247-83.

182
Schieffer, Theodor *Winfrid-Bonifatius und die christliche Grundlegung Europas* (Freiburg B. 1954).
183
Sankt Bonifatius. Gedenkgabe zum zwölfhundertsten Todestag (Fulda 1954)
Cf Maurice Coens in *Analecta Bollandiana* 73 (1955) 462-95.

Carolingians

184
Voigt, Karl *Die karolingische Klosterpolitik und der Niedergang des westfränkischen Königtums: Laienäbte und Klosterinhaber* (KR Abh 90-91; Stuttgart 1917).
185
Semmler, Josef 'Karl der Grosse und das fränkische Mönchtum' *Karl der Grosse. Lebenswerk und Nachleben* ed Wolfgang Braunfels (Düsseldorf 1965-8) II, 255-89.
186
Lesne, Emile 'Les ordonnances monastiques de Louis le Pieux et la *Notitia de servitio monasteriorum*' *Revue d'histoire de l'église de France* 6 (1920) 161-75, 321-38, 449-93.

Benedict of Aniane

Cf **138**.

187
Narberhaus, Josef *Benedikt von Aniane. Werk und Persönlichkeit* (Beiträge 16; Münster W. 1930).
188
Dulcy, Suzanne *La règle de Saint Benoît d'Aniane et la réforme monastique à l'époque carolingienne* (Nîmes 1935).
189
Winandy, Jacques 'L'oeuvre monastique de Saint Benoît d'Aniane' *Mélanges bén* **157**, 237-58.
190
Schmitz, Philibert 'L'influence de Saint Benoît d'Aniane dans l'histoire de

l'ordre de Saint-Benoît' *Monachesimo* **161**, 401-15.

191
Semmler, Josef 'Die Beschlüsse des Aachener Konzils im Jahre 816' *Zs für KG* 74 (1963) 15-82.

192
Pückert, Wilhelm *Aniane und Gellone. Diplomatisch-kritische Untersuchungen zur Geschichte der Reformen des Benedictinerordens im IX. und X. Jahrhundert* (Leipzig 1899).

TENTH TO TWELFTH CENTURIES

General

193
Wolff, Carl 'Die gorzer Reform in ihrem Verhältnis zu deutschen Klöstern' *Elsass-Lothringisches Jahrbuch* 9 (1930) 95-111.

194
Berlière, Ursmer 'L'étude des réformes monastiques des Xe et XIe siècles' *Académie royale de Belgique: Bulletin de la classe des lettres* 5 S, 18 (1932) 137-56.

195
Hallinger, Kassius *Gorze-Kluny. Studien zu den monastischen Lebensformen und Gegensätzen im Hochmittelalter* 2 vols paged consecutively (Stud Ans 22-25; Rome 1950-1)
Among the many reviews and articles to which this work gave rise, see in particular Theodor Schieffer in *Archiv für mittelrheinische Kirchengeschichte* 4 (1952) 24-44; Hubert Dauphin in *Downside Review* 70 (1952) 62-74; Heinrich Büttner in *Aus Mittelalter und Neuzeit (Festschrift Gerhard Kallen)* (Bonn 1957) 17-27.

196
Gérard de Brogne et son oeuvre réformatrice. Etudes publiées à l'occasion du millénaire de sa mort (959-1959) (= *Rev bén* 70.1; Maredsous 1960)
See **373**.

197
Bulst, Neithard *Untersuchungen zu den Klosterreformen Wilhelms von Dijon (962-1031)* (Pariser historische Studien 11; Bonn 1973).

198
Dauphin, Hubert *Le bienheureux Richard, abbé de Saint-Vanne de*

Verdun, †*1046* (Bibliothèque de la Revue d'histoire ecclésiastique 24; Louvain - Paris 1946).

199
McNulty, Patricia and Bernard Hamilton 'Orientale lumen et magistra Latinitas: Greek Influences on Western Monasticism (900-1100)' *Millénaire* **122**, I, 181-216.

200
Wollasch, Joachim *Mönchtum des Mittelalters zwischen Kirche und Welt* (Münstersche Mittelalter-Schriften 7; Munich 1973).

201
Brooke, Christopher *The Monastic World, 1000-1300* (London 1974) With many maps as well as plans and illustrations.

202
Dubois, Jacques 'Les moines dans la société du moyen âge (950-1350)' *Revue d'histoire de l'église de France* 60 (1974) 5-37.

Cluny

Cf **44, 138, 195, 215, 365, 402, 451, 485, 495, 547, 557, 614, 720-4, 783, 831, 851, 866, 923-7, 944, 955.**

203
Sackur, Ernst *Die Cluniacenser in ihrer kirchlichen und allgemeingeschicht- lichen Wirksamkeit bis zur Mitte des elften Jahrhunderts* 2 vols (Halle S. 1892-4).

204
Evans, Joan *Monastic Life at Cluny, 910-1157* (Oxford 1931).

205
Valous, Guy de *Le monachisme clunisien des origines au* XVe *siècle. Vie intérieure des monastères et organisation de l'ordre* 2 vols (Archives 39- 40; Ligugé - Paris 1935; repr with new intro 1970) Cf **721.**

206
A Cluny. Congrès scientifique. Fêtes et cérémonies liturgiques en l'honneur des saints abbés Odon et Odilon 9-11 juillet 1949 (Dijon 1950) See **630.**

207
Violante, Cinzio 'Il monachesimo cluniacense di fronte al mondo politico

ed ecclesiastico (secoli X e XI)' *Spiritualità* 955, 155-242; repr in his
Studi sulla christianità medioevale (Cultura e storia 8; Milan 1972) 3-67.

208
Leclercq, Jean 'Pour une histoire de la vie à Cluny' *Rev d'hist ecc* 57
(1962) 385-408, 783-812; abridged repr in *Sources* 946.

209
Cowdrey, Herbert E. J. *The Cluniacs and the Gregorian Reform* (Oxford
1970).

210
Cluniac Monasticism in the Central Middle Ages ed Noreen Hunt (London
1971)
Collected articles, mostly in translation, by Raffaello Morghen, Kassius
Hallinger, Jacques Hourlier, Kenneth J. Conant, Bernard de Vregille,
Anscari M. Mundó, Hansmartin Schwarzmaier, Joachim Wollasch, Etienne
Delaruelle, and Jean Leclercq (226).

211
*Petrus Venerabilis 1156-1956: Studies and Texts Commemorating the
Eighth Centenary of his Death* ed Giles Constable and James Kritzeck
(Stud Ans 40; Rome 1956)
See 309, 724.

Reform Movements of the Eleventh and Twelfth Centuries

212
Walter, Johannes von *Die ersten Wanderprediger Frankreichs,* I: *Robert
von Arbrissel* (Studien zur Geschichte der Theologie und der Kirche 9.3;
Leipzig 1903) and II: *Bernhard von Thiron; Vitalis von Savigny; Girald von
Salles; Bemerkungen zur Norbert von Xanten und Heinrich von Lausanne*
(Leipzig 1906).

213
Davison, Ellen Scott *Forerunners of Saint Francis and Other Studies* ed
Gertrude R. B. Richards (London 1928)
Includes essays on the Carthusians, Cistercians, Grandmontines, and
Premonstratensians.

214
Tellenbach, Gerd *Libertas. Kirche und Weltordnung im Zeitalter des
Investiturstreites* (Forschungen zur Kirchen- und Geistesgeschichte 7;
Stuttgart 1936; Eng trans by Ralph F. Bennett under the title *Church,
State and Christian Society at the Time of the Investiture Contest* 1940).

215
Ladner, Gerhart *Theologie und Politik vor dem Investiturstreit. Abend-mahlstreit, Kirchenreform, Cluni und Heinrich III.* (Veröffentlichungen des österreichischen Instituts für Geschichtsforschung 2; Baden bei Wien - Brünn - Leipzig - Prague 1936).

216
Werner, Ernst *Die gesellschaftlichen Grundlagen der Klosterreform im 11. Jahrhundert* (Berlin 1953)
Marxist in approach.

217
Werner, Ernst *Pauperes Christi. Studien zu sozial-religiösen Bewegungen im Zeitalter des Reformpapsttums* (Leipzig 1956)
Marxist in approach.

218
Hallinger, Kassius 'Progressi e problemi della ricerca sulla riforma pre-gregoriana' *Monachesimo* **161**, 257-91; German version in *Archiv für mittelrheinische Kirchengeschichte* 9 (1957) 9-32
Criticizes Werner **216**.

219
Chiesa e riforma nella spiritualità del sec. XI (Convegni del Centro di studi sulla spiritualità medievale 6; Todi 1968).

220
I laici nella 'Societas christiana' dei secoli XI e XII. Atti della terza setti-mana internazionale di studio, Mendola, 21-27 agosto 1965 (Pubblicazioni dell'Università cattolica del Sacro Cuore, Contributi 3 S: Varia 5 [Miscellanea del Centro di studi medioevali 5]; Milan 1968)
Includes articles on reformed monks and the laity (Gerd Tellenbach), lay brothers (Jean Leclercq, Jacques Dubois, Cosimo Damiano Fonseca), and women in religious life (Nicolas Huyghebaert).

221
Il monachesimo e la riforma ecclesiastica (1049-1122). Atti della quarta settimana internazionale di studio, Mendola, 23-29 agosto 1968 (Pubbli-cazioni dell'Università cattolica del Sacro Cuore, Contributi 3 S: Varia 7 [Miscellanea del Centro di studi medioevali 6]; Milan 1971)
See **231, 548, 686, 875, 896, 1003** in addition to articles on economy (Georges Duby) and various regions.

The 'Crisis of Cenobitism'

222
Morin, Germain 'Rainaud l'ermite et Ives de Chartres. Un épisode de la crise du cénobitisme au XIe-XIIe siècle' *Rev bén* 40 (1928) 99-115.

223
Dereine, Charles 'Odon de Tournai et la crise du cénobitisme au XIe siècle' *Revue du moyen âge latin* 4 (1948) 137-54.

224
Schmitz, Philibert 'Le monachisme bénédictin au XIIe siècle' *S Bernardo. Pubblicazione commemorativa nell'VIII centenario della sua morte* (Pubblicazioni dell'Università cattolica del Sacro Cuore, NS, 46; Milan 1953) 1-13.

225
Chenu, Marie-Dominique 'Moines, clercs, laïcs au carrefour de la vie évangélique' *Rev d'hist ecc* 69 (1954) 59-89, and in his *La théologie au douzième siècle* (Etudes de philosophie médiévale 45; Paris 1957; Eng trans by Jerome Taylor and Lester K. Little under the title *Nature, Man, and Society in the Twelfth Century* 1968) 225-51.

226
Leclercq, Jean 'La crise du monachisme aux XIe et XIIe siècles' *Bullettino dell'Istituto storico italiano per il medio evo* 70 (1958) 19-41 and in *Témoins* 946; Eng trans in **210**.

227
Cantor, Norman F. 'The Crisis of Western Monasticism, 1050-1130' *American Historical Review* 66 (1960-1) 47-67
Cf **377**.

Camaldoli

Cf **44**, **304**.

228
Mittarelli, Giovanni Benedetto *Annales camaldulenses ordinis S Benedicti* 9 vols (Venice 1755-73).

229
Franke, Walter *Quellen und Chronologie zur Geschichte Romualds von Camaldoli und seiner Einsiedlergenossenschaften im Zeitalter Ottos III.* (Halle S. 1910).

230

Franke, Walter *Romuald von Camaldoli und seine Reformtätigkeit zur Zeit Ottos III.* (Historische Studien, ed Ebering, 107; Berlin 1913).

231

Kurze, Wilhelm 'Campus Malduli. Die Frühgeschichte Camaldolis' *Quellen und Forschungen aus italienischen Archiven und Bibliotheken* 44 (1964) 1-34
Cf also his article in *Monachesimo* **221**, 399-412.

Vallombrosa

Cf **44, 249, 934.**

232

Tarani, Federigo F. *L'ordine vallombrosano. Note storico-cronologiche* (Florence 1921).

233

Quilici, Brunetto 'Giovanni Gualberto e la sua riforma monastica' *Archivio storico italiano* 99.2 [= no 378] (1941) 113-32; 99.3-4 [= nos 379-80] (1941) 27-62; 100.1-2 [= nos 381-2] (1942) 45-99.

234

Boesch Gajano, Sofia 'Storia e tradizione vallombrosane' *Bullettino dell' Istituto storico italiano per il medio evo* 76 (1964) 99-215
Studies sources for history of Vallombrosa in eleventh and early twelfth centuries.

235

Witte, Charles-Martial de 'Les monastères vallombrosains aux XVe et XVIe siècles. Un "status quaestionis"' *Benedictina* 17 (1970) 234-53.

Carthusians

Cf **44, 213, 304, 387, 520, 830, 966, 1000.**

236

Le Couteulx, Charles *Annales ordinis cartusiensis ab anno 1084 ad annum 1429* 8 vols (Montreuil-sur-Mer 1887-91)
Composed at the end of the seventeenth century.

237
Löbbel, Hermann *Der Stifter des Carthäuser-Ordens der heilige Bruno aus Köln* (Kirchengeschichtliche Studien 5.1; Münster W. 1899).

238
Aux sources de la vie cartusienne 6 vols (La Grande Chartreuse 1960-7) By Maurice Laporte, published anonymously and technically for use within the Carthusian order. Vol I: Life of St Bruno; II: Nature of La Chartreuse; III: Lay brothers; IV-VI: *Consuetudines*. Cf the criticisms by Jacques Dubois in *Rev d'hist ecc* 63 (1968) 27-54.

Cistercians

Cf 14-17, 29-32, 44-5, 138, 141, 213, 327-32, 385-6, 392, 397, 440, 444, 471-3, 480, 486, 505, 520, 536, 543, 549, 553, 570-3, 611, 674-84, 695, 708-10, 712, 719, 726, 730, 732-3, 753, 773-5, 789, 830-3, 866, 884, 907, 928-32, 935, 944, 956, 966, 968.

239
Manrique, Angel *Annales cistercienses* 4 vols (Lyon 1642-59) On Manrique and his work, see Maur Cocheril in *Stud mon* 6 (1964) 145-83.

240
Janauschek, Leopold *Originum cisterciensium tomus I* (Vienna 1877) Cf Bruno Schneider in *Cistercienser-Chronik* 73 (1966) 129-37.

241
Arbois de Jubainville, Henri d' *Etudes sur l'état intérieur des abbayes cisterciennes, et principalement de Clairvaux, au XIIe et au XIIIe siècle* (Paris 1858).

242
Müller, Gregor 'Die Entstehung der Charta Charitatis' *Cistercienser-Chronik* 9 (1897) 19-24, 57-61; 'Das Exordium Parvum' *ibid* 311-15, 341-50, 371-8; 'Gründung der Abtei Cîteaux' *ibid* 10 (1898) 1-9, 33-46, 65-76, 97-105; 'Cîteaux unter dem Abte Alberich (1099-1109)' *ibid* 21 (1909) 1-12, 41-50, 75-83, 109-18, 140-53; 'Cîteaux vom Jahre 1109 bis 1119' *ibid* 28 (1916) 1-8, 31-8, 56-62, 86-91, 117-22, 135-42, 161-6, 186-92, 211-16, 227-30; 'Vom Cistercienser Orden' *ibid* 37 (1925) [on 1098-1119] 49-59, 80-8, 106-15, [on 1120-1153] 127-34, 155-63, 176-83, [on 1153-1265] 200-8, 227-35, 248-55, 275-82; *ibid* 38 (1926) [on 1265-

1335] 14-21, 40-8, [on 1335-1493] 68-74, 102-9, 134-40, 159-65, [post-15th century] 197-202, 233-40, 258-64, 289-94, 322-9, 355-63; *ibid* 39 (1927) 17-24, 48-55, 78-85, 115-22, 141-9, 165-72, 200-7, 232-9, 269-73, 303-15

The series *Vom Cistercienser Orden* published together (Bregenz 1927) [not seen]. Together these articles constitute the fullest modern history of the Cistercian order. The first volume, covering 1097-1493, of a revised French translation by Eugène Willems under the title *Esquisse historique de l'ordre de Cîteaux* (Dison-Verviers - Abbaye du Val-Dieu - Paris 1957) was severely criticized by Polykarp Zakar in *Anal cist* 14 (1958) 127-36.

243
Lekai, Louis J. *Les moines blancs. Histoire de l'ordre cistercien* (Paris 1957)
Revised translation by the author of *The White Monks* (1953).

244
Mahn, Jean-Berthold *L'ordre cistercien et son gouvernement des origines au milieu du XIIIe siècle (1098-1265)* (Bibliothèque des Ecoles françaises d'Athènes et de Rome 161; Paris 1945).

245
Dimier, Marie-Anselme *Saint Louis et Cîteaux* (Paris 1954).

246
Mahn, Jean-Berthold *Le pape Benoît XII et les cisterciens* (Bibliothèque de l'Ecole des hautes études 295; Paris 1949).

Origins

247
Berlière, Ursmer 'Les origines de Cîteaux et l'ordre bénédictin au XIIe siècle' *Rev d'hist ecc* 1 (1900) 448-71; 2 (1901) 253-90; and separately (Louvain 1901).

248
[Ducourneau], J. Othon 'Les origines cisterciennes' *Rev Mab* 22 (1932) 133-64, 233-52; 23 (1933) 1-32, 81-111, 153-89
Cf Jacques Laurent in *Annales de Bourgogne* 6 (1934) 213-29.

249
Duvernay, Roger 'Cîteaux, Vallombreuse et Etienne Harding' *Anal cist* 8 (1952) 379-495.

250

'Chronique de la Section d'histoire du droit et des institutions de Bourgogne et de Suisse romande au Congrès bourguignon des sociétés savantes, tenu à Dijon en 1953. I: Les débuts des abbayes cisterciennes dans le duché de Bourgogne et la Lingonie. II: Les débuts des abbayes cisterciennes dans le comté de Bourgogne. III: Les abbayes cisterciennes dans la Suisse romande' *Mémoires de la Société pour l'histoire du droit et des institutions des anciens pays bourguignons, comtois et romands* 15 (1953) 51-199 Cf 258.

251

Lefèvre, Jean-A. 'Que savons-nous du Cîteaux primitif?' *Rev d'hist ecc* 51 (1956) 5-41 Summarizes the conclusions of his seven articles in *Coll cist* 16-17 (1954-55). Cf Alain d'Herblay in *Rev d'hist ecc* 50 (1955) 158-64; Jacques Winandy in *Rev bén* 67 (1957) 49-76; David Knowles in *Hist Enterprises* 135, 199-224, with a bibliography of Lefèvre's work to date.

252

Van Damme, Jean-B. 'Autour des origines cisterciennes' *Coll cist* 20 (1958) 37-60, 153-68, 374-90; 21 (1959) 70-86, 137-56, and separately ([Westmalle] [1959]) Cf Van Damme's later articles in *Cîteaux* 12 (1961) 28-60; *Stud mon* 4 (1962) 111-37; *Anal cist* 19 (1963) 51-104; *Anal cist* 21 (1965) 128-37.

253

Schneider, Bruno 'Cîteaux und die benediktinische Tradition' *Anal cist* 16 (1960) 169-254; 17 (1961) 73-114.

254

Zakar, Polykarp 'Die Anfänge des Zisterzienserordens. Kurze Bemerkungen zu den Studien der letzten zehn Jahre' *Anal cist* 20 (1964) 103-38; and 'Réponse aux "Quelques à-propos" du P. Van Damme sur les origines cisterciennes. Quelques conclusions' *ibid* 21 (1965) 138-66.

255

Leclercq, Jean 'The Intentions of the Founders of the Cistercian Order' *The Cistercian Spirit: A Symposium in Memory of Thomas Merton* ed M. Basil Pennington (Cistercian Studies Series 3; Spencer, Mass. 1970) 88-133.

Bernard of Clairvaux

Cf **15-17**, **138**, **224**, **271**, **675**, **953**.

256
Saint Bernard et son temps 2 vols (Association bourguignonne des sociétés savantes: Congrès de 1927; Dijon 1928-9)
See **572**, **774**.

257
Bernard de Clairvaux (Commission d'histoire de l'ordre de Cîteaux 3; Paris 1953).

258
Mélanges Saint Bernard. XXIVe Congrès de l'Association bourguignonne des sociétés savantes, Dijon 1953 (8e centenaire de la mort de Saint Bernard) (Dijon 1954)
Cf **250**.

259
Leclercq, Jean *Recueil d'études sur Saint Bernard et ses écrits* 3 vols (Storia e letteratura 92, 104, 114; Rome 1962-9).

Other Orders and Centres of Reform

La Chaise-Dieu

260
Gaussin, Pierre-Roger *L'abbaye de La Chaise-Dieu (1043-1518). L'abbaye en Auvergne et son rayonnement dans la Chrétienté* (Paris 1962).

Fontevrault

Cf **212**.

261
Niderst, René *Robert d'Arbrissel et les origines de l'ordre de Fontevrault* (Rodez 1952).

Grandmont

Cf **213**, **365**, **933**.

262

Becquet, Jean 'Les institutions de l'ordre de Grandmont au moyen âge' *Rev Mab* 42 (1952) 31-42
Cf his other articles on the order of Grandmont in *Rev Mab* 43-53 (1953-63) and *Bulletin de la Société archéologique et historique du Limousin* 86-87 (1955-60).

Molesme

263

Laurent, Jacques *Cartulaires de l'abbaye de Molesme* 2 vols (Collection de documents publiés avec le concours de la Commission des antiquités de la Côte-d'Or 1; Paris 1907-11)
I, 111-275, on Molesme and its order.

Montevergine

264

Mongelli, Giovanni *Storia de Montevergine e della congregazione verginiana* 6 vols (Avellino 1965-71)
Vol I goes from twelfth century to 1430.

Pulsano

265

Angelillis, Ciro 'Pulsano e l'ordine monastico pulsanese' *Archivio storico pugliese* 6 (1953) 421-66.

Savigny

Cf 212.

266

Auvry, Claude *Histoire de la congrégation de Savigny* 3 vols (Rouen - Paris 1896-8)
Written in the seventeenth century.

267

[Rambaud-] Buhot, Jacqueline 'L'abbaye normande de Savigny, chef d'ordre et fille de Cîteaux' *Le Moyen Âge* 46 (3 S, 7; 1936) 1-19, 104-21, 178-90, 249-72.

Sempringham

Cf **830**.

268
Graham, Rose *S Gilbert of Sempringham and the Gilbertines: A History of the Only English Monastic Order* (London 1901).

Siegburg

269
Semmler, Josef *Die Klosterreform von Siegburg. Ihre Ausbreitung und ihr Reformprogramm im 11. und 12. Jahrhundert* (Rheinisches Archiv 53; Bonn 1959).

Williamites

270
Elm, Kaspar *Beiträge zur Geschichte des Wilhelmitenordens* (Münstersche Forschungen 14; Cologne - Graz 1962).

THIRTEENTH TO FIFTEENTH CENTURIES

General

271
Coulton, George Gordon *Five Centuries of Religion* 4 vols 2nd ed of I (Cambridge Studies in Medieval Life and Thought; Cambridge 1929-50) Vol I: *St Bernard, his Predecessors and Successors, 1000-1200 AD*; II: *The Friars and the Dead Weight of Tradition, 1200-1400 AD*; III: *Getting and Spending*; IV: *The Last Days of Medieval Monachism.*

272
Delaruelle, Etienne, Edmond-René Labande, and Paul Ourliac *L'église au temps du Grand Schisme et de la crise conciliaire (1378-1449)* 2 vols paged consecutively (Histoire de l'église 47, XIV.1-2; Paris 1962-4)
Especially pp 1031-63 on the reform of old monastic orders.

273
Hourlier, Jacques *L'âge classique (1140-1378).* *Les religieux* (Histoire du droit et des institutions de l'église en Occident 10; [Paris] 1974).

274
Hofmeister, Philipp 'Abtei und Celle im späteren Mittelalter' *Historisches Jahrbuch* 72 (1953) 222-37.

Orders and Centres of Reform

Celestines

275
Frugoni, Arsenio *Celestiniana* (Istituto storico italiano per il medio evo: Studi storici 6-7; Rome 1954).

276
Moscati, Anna 'I monasteri di Pietro Celestino' *Bullettino dell'Istituto storico italiano per il medio evo* 68 (1956) 91-163.

Monte Oliveto

277
Lugano, Placido M. 'Inizi e primi sviluppi dell'istituzione di Monte Oliveto (1313-1348)' *Benedictina* 1 (1947) 43-81.

278
Scarpini, Modesto *I monaci benedettini di Monte Oliveto* (Alessandria 1952)
Pp 7-122 from the foundation to 1501.

279
Picasso, Giorgio M. 'Aspetti e problemi della storia della congregazione benedettina de Monte Oliveto' *Stud mon* 3 (1961) 383-408.

S Giustina, Padua

280
Leccisotti, Tommaso 'La congregazione benedettina di S Giustina e la riforma della chiesa al secolo XV' *Archivio della r. deputazione romana di storia patria* 67 (NS, 10; 1944) 451-69.

281

Tassi, Ildefonso *Ludovico Barbo (1381-1443)* (Uomini e dottrine 1; Rome 1952).

Bursfeld

Cf **44**.

282

Linneborn, Johannes 'Die bursfelder Kongregation während der ersten hundert Jahre ihres Bestehens' *Deutsche Geschichtsblätter* 14 (1912-13) 3-30, 33-58.

283

Hofmeister, Philipp 'Die Verfassung der bursfelder Kongregation' *Stud Mitt* 53 (1935) 37-76.

284

Volk, Paul *Urkunden zur Geschichte der bursfelder Kongregation* (Kanonistische Studien und Texte 20; Bonn 1951)

Pp 3-51 is introduction on the history and privileges of the order.

285

Dörries, Hermann 'Bursfelde und seine Reform' *Wort und Stunde* 132, II, 295-321.

Western Monasticism:
Special Topics

CANONS

Cf 44, 141, 343-6, 388-9, 436-8, 440, 474-6, 481, 502, 520, 544, 558, 562, 754-9, 868, 874, 918, 957, 989, 996-7.

General

286
Dereine, Charles 'Chanoines (des origines au XIIIe s.)' *Dictionnaire d'histoire* **40**, XII (1953) 353-405.

287
Poggiaspalla, Ferminio *La vita comune del clero dalle origini alla riforma gregoriana* (Uomini e dottrine 14; Rome 1968).

288
Fonseca, Cosimo Damiano *Medioevo canonicale* (Pubblicazioni dell' Università cattolica del Sacro Cuore, Contributi 3 S: Scienze storiche 12; Milan 1970)
Part I (pp 5-71) is an historiographical survey of the development of an awareness of the historical importance of canons; part II (pp 75-189) deals with manuscript collections of canonical statutes and regulations.

289
Hertling, Ludwig 'Kanoniker, Augustinusregel und Augustinerorden' *Zs für katholische Theologie* **54** (1930) 335-59.

290
Saint Chrodegang. Communications présentées au colloque tenu à Metz à l'occasion du douzième centenaire de sa mort (Metz 1967)
See **758**.

291
Dereine, Charles 'Vie commune, règle de Saint Augustin et chanoines
réguliers au XIe siècle' *Rev d'hist ecc* 41 (1946) 365-406
On this and other works by Dereine see Jean-François Lemarignier in
Revue d'histoire de l'église de France 35 (1949) 36-8.

292
*La vita comune del clero nei secoli XI e XII. Atti della settimana di studio,
Mendola, settembre 1959* 2 vols (Pubblicazioni dell'Università cattolica
del Sacro Cuore, 3 S: Scienze storiche 2-3 [Miscellanea del Centro di studi
medioevali 3]; Milan 1962)
Includes articles on economic life (Georges Duby), spirituality (Jean
Leclercq, Etienne Delaruelle), liturgy (Enrico Cattaneo), Premonstratensians
(François Petit), and on various regions.

Premonstratensians

Cf 33, 44, 141, 212-13, 292, 343, 389, 681-2, 830, 834, 866, 958-9.

293
Backmund, Norbert *Monasticon praemonstratense* 3 vols (Straubing
1949-56)
Vol I: Germany, Switzerland, Scandinavia, Poland, Bohemia, Austria,
Hungary, Italy, Levant; II: Great Britain, Ireland, Netherlands, Belgium,
Northern France; III: Remainder of France, Spain, Portugal, America. Cf
Maur Cocheril in *Stud mon* 1 (1959) 423-36.

294
Hugo, Charles L. *Sacri et canonici ordinis praemonstratensis annales* 1 vol
in 2 (Nancy 1734-6).

295
Dereine, Charles 'Les origines de Prémontré' *Rev d'hist ecc* 42 (1947)
352-78.

Other Orders

Arrouaise

296
Milis, Ludo[vicus] *L'ordre des chanoines réguliers d'Arrouaise. Son histoire*

et son organisation, de la fondation de l'abbaye-mère (vers 1090) à la fin des chapitres annuels (1471) 2 vols (Rijksuniversiteit te Gent: Werken uitgegeven door de faculteit van de letteren en Wijsbegeerte 147-148; Bruges 1969) Vol I: Text; II: Maps.

L'Artige

297
Becquet, Jean 'Aux origines du prieuré de l'Artige, chef d'ordre canonial en Limousin (XIIe et XIIIe s.)' *Bulletin de la Société archéologique et historique du Limousin* 90 (1963) 85-100; and 'L'ordre de l'Artige' *ibid* 97 (1970) 83-142.

Aureil

298
Becquet, Jean 'La vie de Saint Gaucher, fondateur des chanoines réguliers d'Aureil en Limousin' *Rev Mab* 54 (1964) 25-55
Cf other articles on this order by Becquet in *Bulletin de la Société archéologique et historique du Limousin* 91-99 (1964-72).

Rottenbuch

299
Mois, Jakob *Das Stift Rottenbuch in der Kirchenreform des XI.-XII. Jahrhunderts. Ein Beitrag zur Ordens-Geschichte der Augustiner-Chorherren* (Beiträge zur altbayerischen Kirchengeschichte, 3 S, 19; Munich 1953).

St Rufus

300
Carrier de Belleuse, Albert *Liste des abbayes, chapitres, prieurés, églises de l'ordre de Saint-Ruf* (Etudes et documents sur l'ordre de Saint-Ruf 1; Romans 1933).

HERMITS AND RECLUSES

General

Cf **560**.

301

Gougaud, Louis *Ermites et reclus. Etudes sur d'anciennes formes de vie religieuse* (Moines et monastères 5; Ligugé 1928) Cf the supplementary bibliography for 1928-33 in *Rev bén* 45 (1933) 281-91.

302

Anson, Peter F. *The Call of the Desert: The Solitary Life in the Christian Church* (1932) 2nd ed (London 1964) First edition entitled *The Quest of Solitude*. Comes down to modern times.

303

Leclercq, Jean 'L'érémitisme en Occident jusqu'à l'an mil' *Millénaire* **122**, I, 161-80 and *Eremitismo* **304**, 27-44.

304

L'eremitismo in Occidente nei secoli XI e XII. Atti della seconda settimana internazionale di studio, Mendola, 30 agosto - 6 settembre 1962 (Pubblicazioni dell'Università cattolica del Sacro Cuore, Contributi 3 S: Varia 4 [Miscellanea del Centro di studi medioevali 4]; Milan 1965) See **303**, **529**; also articles on Camaldoli (Giovanni Tabacco), Carthusians (Bernard Bligny), and various regions.

305

Bosl, Karl ' ''ΕΡΗΜΟΣ - eremus. Begriffsgeschichtliche Bemerkungen zum historischen Problem der Entfremdung und Vereinsamung des Menschen' *Polychordia: Festschrift Franz Dölger zum 75. Geburtstag* ed Peter Wirth (Byzantinische Forschungen 2; Amsterdam 1967) 73-90.

Regional

England

306

Clay, Rotha Mary *The Hermits and Anchorites of England* (London 1914) Cf two supplementary articles in *Journal of the British Archaeological*

Association 3 S, 16 (1953) 74-86 and *Archaeologia Aeliana* 4 S, 33 (1955) 202-17.
307
Darwin, Francis D. S. *The English Mediaeval Recluse* (London [1944]).

France

308
Raison, L. and René Niderst 'Le mouvement érémitique dans l'ouest de la France à la fin du XIe siècle et au début du XIIe' *Annales de Bretagne* 55 (1948) 1-46.
309
Leclercq, Jean 'Pierre le Vénérable et l'érémitisme clunisien' *Petrus Venerabilis* 211, 99-120.

Germany

310
Doerr, Otmar *Das Institut der Inclusen in Süddeutschland* (Beiträge 18; Münster W. 1934).
311
Grundmann, Herbert 'Deutsche Eremiten, Einsiedler und Klausner im Hochmittelalter (10.-12. Jahrhundert)' *Archiv für Kulturgeschichte* 45 (1963) 60-90.

Spain

312
Díaz y Díaz, Manuel C. 'El eremitismo en la España visigótica' *Revista portuguesa de história* 6 (1955) 217-37; Eng trans in *Classical Folia* 23 (1969) 209-27.
313
España eremitica. Actas de la VI semana de estudios monásticos, Abadía de San Salvador de Leyre, 15-20 de septiembre de 1963 (Analecta legerensia 1; Pamplona 1970)
26 articles on eremitism in Spain from Roman times to the eighteenth century, mostly on various regions.

WOMEN IN RELIGIOUS LIFE

General

Cf **153, 220, 556, 895, 967.**

314

Tamburini, Ascanio *De jure abbatissarum et monialium; sive Praxis gubernandi moniales, aliasque mulieres sub habitu ecclesiastico, et regulari degentes* (Rome 1638)
It later appeared as vol IV of the 1691 edition of **593.**

315

Eckenstein, Lina *Woman under Monasticism: Chapters on Saint-Lore and Convent Life between AD 500 and AD 1500* (Cambridge 1896).

316

Hofmeister, Philipp 'Von den Nonnenklöstern' *Archiv für katholisches Kirchenrecht* 114 (1934) 3-96, 353-437
Sections on vows, clausura, jurisdiction, superiors, etc; mostly medieval but some modern.

317

Hilpisch, Stephanus *Geschichte der Benediktinerinnen* (Benediktinisches Geistesleben 3; St Ottilien 1951; Eng trans by M. Joanne Muggli 1958).

318

Bernards, Matthäus *Speculum virginum. Geistigkeit und Seelenleben der Frau im Hochmittelalter* (Forschungen zur Volkskunde 36-38; Cologne - Graz 1955); and 'Zur Seelsorge in den Frauenklöstern des Hochmittelalters' *Rev bén* 66 (1956) 256-68.

319

Rambaud-Buhot, Jacqueline 'Le statut des moniales chez les pères de l'église, dans les règles monastiques et les collections canoniques, jusqu'au XIIe siècle' *Sainte Fare et Faremoutiers* (Abbaye de Faremoutiers 1956) 149-74.

320

Fontette, Micheline de *Les religieuses à l'âge classique du droit canon. Recherches sur les structures juridiques des branches féminines des ordres* (Bibliothèque de la Société d'histoire ecclésiastique de la France; Paris 1967).

321
Prager, Mirjam *Die religiösen Frauenorden* (Aschaffenburg 1968)
Not seen.

Consecrated Virgins

Cf 803-4.

322
Wilpert, Joseph *Die gottgeweihten Jungfrauen in den ersten Jahrhunderten der Kirche* (Freiburg B. 1892)
Includes chapter on beginnings of monastic life.

323
Koch, Hugo *Virgines Christi. Die Gelübde der gottgeweihten Jungfrauen in den ersten drei Jahrhunderten* (Texte und Untersuchungen zur Geschichte der altchristlichen Literatur 31.2; Leipzig 1907).

324
Oppenheim, Philipp *Die consecratio virginum als geistesgeschichtliches Problem. Eine Studie zu ihrem Aufbau, ihrem Wert und ihrer Geschichte* (Rome 1943).

325
Metz, René *La consécration des vierges dans l'église romaine. Etude d'histoire de la liturgie* (Bibliothèque de l'Institut de droit canonique de l'Université de Strasbourg 4; Paris 1954)
From early Christian times to the sixteenth century.

326
Metz, René 'La consécration des vierges dans l'église franque du VIIe au IXe siècle' *Revue des sciences religieuses* 31 (1957) 105-21; and 'La consécration des vierges dans l'église franque d'après le plus ancienne vie de sainte Pusinne (VIIIe-IXe siècle)' *ibid* 35 (1961) 32-48.

Cistercians

327
Luddy, Ailbe J. *The Cistercian Nuns. A Brief Sketch of the History of the Order from its Foundation to the Present Day* (Dublin 1931)
Mostly modern; no notes.

328
Roisin, Simone 'L'efflorescence cistercienne et le courant féminin de piété au XIIIe siècle' *Rev d'hist ecc* 39 (1943) 342-78.

329
Krenig, Ernst 'Mittelalterliche Frauenklöster nach den Konstitutionen von Cîteaux' *Anal cist* 10 (1954) 1-105.

330
Boyd, Catherine E. *A Cistercian Nunnery in Mediaeval Italy: The Story of Rifreddo in Saluzzo, 1220-1300* (Harvard Historical Monographs 18; Cambridge, Mass. 1943).

331
Griesser, Bruno 'Stephan Lexington, Abt von Savigny, als Visitator der ihm unterstehenden Frauenklöster' *Cistercienser-Chronik* 67 (1960) 14-34.

332
Lepointe, Gabriel 'Réflexions sur des textes concernant la propriété individuelle de religieuses cisterciennes dans la région lilloise' *Rev d'hist ecc* 49 (1954) 743-69
Mostly on fourteenth to fifteenth centuries.

Bridgettines

333
Nyberg, Tore *Birgittinische Klostergründungen des Mittelalters* (Bibliotheca historica lundensis 15; Lund 1965).

334
Cnattingius, Hans J. *Studies in the Order of St Bridget of Sweden, 1: The Crisis in the 1420's* (Acta universitatis stockholmiensis 7; Stockholm - Göteborg - Uppsala 1963).

Regional

335
Fiey, Jean Maurice 'Cénobitisme féminin ancien dans les églises syriennes orientale et occidentale' *L'Orient syrien* 10 (1965) 281-306
See also, on Byzantine nuns, Janin **81**, 36-42.

336
Aigrain, René *Sainte Radegonde (vers 520-587)* (Paris 1918)
Has chapters on the monastery at Poitiers and the Rule of St Caesarius.

337
Hamilton, Bernard 'The House of Theophylact and the Promotion of the Religious Life among Women in Tenth Century Rome' *Stud mon* 12 (1970) 195-217
Cf **517**.

338
Power, Eileen *Medieval English Nunneries, c. 1275 to 1535* (Cambridge 1922).

339
Paschini, Pio 'I monasteri femminili in Italia nel '500' *Problemi di vita religiosa in Italia nel Cinquecento. Atti del Convegno di storia della chiesa in Italia (Bologna, 2-6 sett 1958)* (Padua 1960) 31-60.

340
Spahr, Kolumban 'Nikolaus von Cues, das adelige Frauenstift Sonnenburg OSB und die mittelalterliche Nonnenklausur' *Cusanus Gedächtnisschrift* ed Nikolaus Grass (Innsbruck - Munich 1970) 307-26.

Beguines

341
Greven, Joseph *Die Anfänge der Beginen. Ein Beitrag zur Geschichte der Volksfrömmigkeit und des Ordenswesens im Hochmittelalter* (Vorreformationsgeschichtliche Forschungen 8; Münster W. 1912).

342
McDonnell, Ernest W. *The Beguines and Beghards in Medieval Culture, with Special Emphasis on the Belgian Scene* (New Brunswick 1954).

Canonesses

Cf **558**.

Regular

343
Erens, Ambrosius 'Les soeurs dans l'ordre de Prémontré' *Anal praem* 5 (1929) 5-26.

Secular

344
Schaefer, Karl Heinrich *Die Kanonissenstifter im deutschen Mittelalter.
Ihre Entwicklung und innere Einrichtung im Zusammenhang mit dem altchristlichen Sanktimonialentum* (KR Abh 43-44; Stuttgart 1907)
Cf the criticisms of Wilhelm Levison in *Westdeutsche Zs* 27 (1908) 491-
512; reprinted in his *Aus rheinischer und fränkischer Frühzeit* (Düsseldorf
1948) 489-511.

345
Despy, Georges 'Les chapitres de chanoinesses nobles en Belgique au
moyen âge' *Fédération archéologique et historique de Belgique: XXXVIe
congrès (1955): Annales* 2: *Communications* (Ghent 1956) 169-79.

346
Gampl, Inge *Adelige Damenstifte. Untersuchungen zur Entstehung adeliger
Damenstifte in Österreich unter besonderer Berücksichtigung der alten
Kanonissenstifte Deutschlands und Lothringens* (Wiener rechtsgeschicht-
liche Arbeiten 5; Vienna - Munich 1960).

Double Monasteries

Cf **261**, **268**.

347
Bateson, Mary 'Origin and Early History of Double Monasteries' *Trans-
actions of the Royal Historical Society* NS, 13 (1899) 137-98
Covers fourth to ninth centuries.

348
Pargoire, Jules 'Les monastères doubles chez les Byzantins' *Echos d'Orient*
9 (1906) 21-5
Cf Janin **81**, 42-4 and Mahfoud **106**, 289-315.

349
Thompson, Alexander Hamilton 'Double Monasteries and the Male
Element in Nunneries' *The Ministry of Women: A Report by a Committee
Appointed by His Grace the Lord Archbishop of Canterbury* (London
1919) Appendix VIII (145-64)
Studies England from the seventh to the sixteenth centuries.

350

Berlière, Ursmer *Les monastères doubles aux XIIe et XIIIe siècles* (Académie royale de Belgique. Classe des lettres et des sciences morales et politiques: Mémoires in -8°, 2 S, 18.3; Brussels 1923).

351

Hilpisch, Stephanus *Die Doppelklöster. Entstehung und Organisation* (Beiträge 15; Münster W. 1928).

352

Bühler, Irma 'Forschungen über Benediktiner-Doppelklöster im heutigen Bayern' *Zs für bayerische Kirchengeschichte* 3 (1928) 197-207; 4 (1929) 1-13, 199-229; 5 (1930) 17-33, 229-251.

353

Orlandis, José 'Los monasterios dúplices españoles en la alta edad media' *Anuario de historia del derecho español* 30 (1960) 49-88, and in his *Estudios* **487**, 167-202

Covers seventh to eleventh centuries.

Western Monasticism: Regional

Maps

354

Ryan, Alice Mary *A Map of Old English Monasteries and Related Ecclesiastical Foundations AD 400-1066* (Cornell Studies in English 28; Ithaca, N.Y. 1939)
Includes brief introduction, bibliography, and index.

355

Map of Monastic Britain published by the Ordnance Survey (1950) 2nd ed 2 sheets (Chessington, Surrey 1954-5).

356

Léarscáilíocht Eireann. Map of Monastic Ireland ed Richard Neville Hadcock (1959) 2nd ed (Dublin 1965)
Also published with **362**.

Repertories

357

Dugdale, William *Monasticon anglicanum: A History of the Abbies and other Monasteries, Hospitals, Frieries, and Cathedral and Collegiate Churches, with their Dependencies, in England and Wales* (1655-73) ed John Caley, Henry Ellis, and Bulkeley Bandinel. 6 vols in 8 (London 1817-30 and 1846)
Vols I-IV: Benedictine houses; V: Cluniacs and Cistercians; VI.1: Carthusians and Augustinians; VI.2: Other orders; VI.3: Canons, friars, etc.

358
Tanner, Thomas *Notitia monastica; or, An Account of all the Abbies, Priories, and Houses of Friers, formerly in England and Wales* (1744) ed James Nasmith (Cambridge 1787).

359
Archdall, Mervyn *Monasticon hibernicum: or, A History of the Abbeys, Priories, and Other Religious Houses in Ireland* (1786) ed Patrick Moran 2 vols (Dublin 1873-6)
The third volume, announced on the title page, was never published.

360
Knowles, David and Richard Neville Hadcock *Medieval Religious Houses: England and Wales* (1953) 2nd ed (London 1971)
Based on David Knowles *The Religious Houses of Medieval England* (London 1940).

361
Easson, David E. *Medieval Religious Houses: Scotland* (London - New York - Toronto 1957)
With a foreword by David Knowles and maps by Richard Neville Hadcock.

362
Gwynn, Aubrey O. and Richard Neville Hadcock *Medieval Religious Houses: Ireland* (London 1970)
With map of monastic Ireland **356** as supplement.

England

Cf **5, 166, 268, 306-7, 338, 349, 432, 550-1, 577, 677-80, 688, 690, 698, 700, 705-13, 818, 845, 864, 869, 883, 908, 915-18, 969**.

363
Taunton, Ethelred L. *The English Black Monks of St Benedict: A Sketch of their History from the Coming of St Augustine to the Present Day* 2 vols (London 1897)
Vol I comes down to 1601.

364
Gasquet, Francis Aidan *English Monastic Life* (1904) 6th ed (London 1924).

365
Graham, Rose *English Ecclesiastical Studies: Being Some Essays in Research*

in Medieval History (London 1929)
Includes articles on the Cluniacs and Grandmontines in England.
366
Smith, Reginald A. L. *Collected Papers* (London - New York - Toronto
1947)
Includes essays on English monastic financial administration and on 'The
Benedictine Contribution to Medieval English Agriculture'.
367
Dickinson, John C. *Monastic Life in Medieval England* (London 1961).
368
Thompson, Alexander Hamilton 'Northumbrian Monasticism' *Bede: His
Life, Times and Writings. Essays in Commemoration of the Twelfth Centenary of his Death* ed Alexander Hamilton Thompson (Oxford 1935)
60-101.
369
Knowles, David *The Monastic Order in England: A History of its Development from the Times of St Dunstan to the Fourth Lateran Council, 940-1216* (1940) 2nd ed (Cambridge 1963)
Continued by **376**.
370
Knowles, David, Christopher N. L. Brooke, and Vera C. M. London *The
Heads of Religious Houses: England and Wales, 940-1216* (Cambridge
1972).
371
Robinson, Joseph Armitage *The Times of Saint Dunstan* (Ford Lectures
1922; Oxford 1923)
Chapters on Dunstan, Ethelwold, Oswald, and the *Regularis concordia*.
372
Regularis concordia ed and trans Thomas Symons (London - Edinburgh,
etc 1953)
See introduction, pp ix-xliv, on the revival and organization of monasticism
in England in the tenth century.
373
Dauphin, Hubert 'Le renouveau monastique en Angleterre au Xe siècle et
ses rapports avec la réforme de Saint Gérard de Brogne' *Gérard* **196**, 177-96
Cf the comment by Eric John, *ibid* 197-203, saying that 'the insular
character of the reform movement has been much exaggerated'; and the
reply to John by Thomas Symons in *Downside Review* 80 (1962) 55-69.

374

John, Eric *Orbis Britanniae and Other Studies* (Studies in Early English History 4; Leicester 1966)
Includes among others essays on the tenth-century monastic reform in England.

375

Southern, Richard W. *Saint Anselm and his Biographer: A Study of Monastic Life and Thought, 1059-c.1130* (Birkbeck Lectures 1959; Cambridge 1963)
Includes chapters on 'The Monk of Bec' and 'The Community at Canterbury'.

376

Knowles, David *The Religious Orders in England* 3 vols (Cambridge 1948-59)
Continuation of **369**. Vol I: 1216-1340; II: The End of the Middle Ages; III: The Tudor Age, on which cf Henry O. Evennett in *Stud mon* 2 (1960) 387-419.

377

Bethell, Denis L. 'English Black Monks and Episcopal Elections in the 1120s' *English Historical Review* 84 (1969) 673-98
In part replies to Cantor **227**.

378

Pantin, William A. 'The General and Provincial Chapters of the English Black Monks, 1215-1540' *Transactions of the Royal Historical Society* 4 S, 10 (1927) 195-263
Cf the bibliography of Pantin's works in *Ampleforth Journal* 79.1 (1974) 107-10 and 79.2 (1974) 137.

379

Hofmeister, Philipp 'Die Verfassung der mittelalterlichen englischen Benediktinerkongregation' *Stud Mitt* 71 (1960) 39-68.

380

Moorman, John R. H. *Church Life in England in the Thirteenth Century* (Cambridge 1945)
Part II (pp 242-401) on monasteries.

381

Cheney, Christopher R. *Episcopal Visitation of Monasteries in the Thirteenth Century* (Publications of the University of Manchester 211: Historical Series 58; Manchester 1931).

382

Wood, Susan M. *English Monasteries and their Patrons in the Thirteenth Century* (Oxford Historical Series; Oxford 1955).

383

Morgan [Chibnall], Marjorie M. 'The Suppression of the Alien Priories' *History* 26 (1941) 204-12.

384

Dobson, Richard B. *Durham Priory, 1400-1450* (Cambridge Studies in Medieval Life and Thought, 3 S, 6; Cambridge 1973).

Cistercians and Carthusians

385

Mullin, Francis A. *A History of the Work of the Cistercians in Yorkshire (1131-1300)* (Washington 1932)
Includes chapters on economic activities and cultural and social influence.

386

Hill, Bennett D. *English Cistercian Monasteries and their Patrons in the Twelfth Century* (Urbana, Ill. 1968).

387

Thompson, E. Margaret *The Carthusian Order in England* (Church Historical Society Publications, NS, 3; London 1930).

Canons

388

Dickinson, John C. *The Origins of the Austin Canons and their Introduction into England* (London 1950).

389

Colvin, Howard M. *The White Canons in England* (Oxford 1951).

Scotland

390

Coulton, George Gordon *Scottish Abbeys and Social Life* (Cambridge Studies in Medieval Life and Thought; Cambridge 1933).

Wales

Cf 44, 712.

391
Williams, Glanmor *The Welsh Church from Conquest to Reformation* (Cardiff 1962)
Includes much material, especially pp 345-413, on monasteries.
392
O'Sullivan, Jeremiah F. *Cistercian Settlements in Wales and Monmouthshire, 1140-1540* (Fordham University Studies: History Series 2; New York 1947).

Ireland

Cf 7, 749, 909, 919.

393
Ryan, John *Irish Monasticism: Origins and Early Development* (London - New York - Toronto 1931; repr with new intro and bibliography 1972)
Cf Louis Gougaud in *Studies* 20 (1931) 195-208.
394
Adomnan's Life of Columba ed and trans Alan O. Anderson and Marjorie O. Anderson (London - Edinburgh, etc 1961)
Introduction, pp 30-124, covers Columba, Iona, and the historical background of Irish monasticism.
395
Hughes, Kathleen *The Church in Early Irish Society* (London 1966)
Goes down to the twelfth century, with several chapters on monasticism.
396
Bethell, Denis 'English Monks and Irish Reform in the Eleventh and Twelfth Centuries' *Historical Studies* 8 (1969) 111-35.
397
Watt, John A. *The Church and the Two Nations in Medieval Ireland* (Cambridge Studies in Medieval Life and Thought, 3 S, 3; Cambridge 1970)
Pp 85-108 deal especially with the Cistercians.

Irish Monks on the Continent

Cf **177-80**.

398

Gougaud, Louis 'L'oeuvre des *Scotti* dans l'Europe continentale (fin VIe-fin XIe siècles)' *Rev d'hist ecc* 9 (1908) 21-37, 255-77.

399

Gougaud, Louis *Les saints irlandais hors d'Irlande étudiés dans le culte et dans la dévotion traditionelle* (Bibliothèque de la Revue d'histoire ecclésiastique 16; Louvain - Oxford 1936).

400

Fuhrmann, Joseph P. *Irish Medieval Monasteries on the Continent* (Washington 1927)
Covers seventh to fifteenth centuries.

401

Bittermann, Helen Robbins 'The Influence of Irish Monks on Merovingian Diocesan Organization' *American Historical Review* 40 (1935) 232-45.

402

Gwynn, Aubrey O. 'Irish Monks and the Cluniac Reform' *Studies* 29 (1940) 409-30.

403

Gwynn, Aubrey O. 'Ireland and the Continent in the Eleventh Century' *Irish Historical Studies* 8 (1953) 193-216.

404

Gwynn, Aubrey O. 'Some Notes on the History of the Irish and Scottish Benedictine Monasteries in Germany' *Innes Review* 5 (1954) 5-27
Covers twelfth to twentieth centuries.

405

Bischoff, Bernhard 'Il monachesimo irlandese nei suoi rapporti col Continente' *Monachesimo* **161**, 121-38.

406

Ó Fiaich, Tomás 'Irish Peregrini on the Continent: Recent Research in Germany' *Irish Ecclesiastical Record* 103 (1965) 233-40.

FRANCE

Cf 4, 212, 250, 297-8, 308-9, 332, 336, 383, 569, 573, 603, 623, 629-30, 634, 642-5, 655, 662-3, 672, 681-3, 687, 696-7, 714-24, 748, 750, 821, 861, 871, 887, 898, 914, 923-8, 933, 970.

Repertories

407
Gallia christiana (1626) 2nd ed by Scévole and Louis de Sainte-Marthe 4 vols (Paris 1656). 3rd ed by Denis de Sainte-Marthe [I-III], the Benedictines of St Maur [IV-XIII], and Barthélemy Hauréau [XIV-XVI] (Paris 1715-1865); continued and supplemented by *Gallia christiana novissima* ed Joseph H. Albanès et al, 7 vols (Montbéliard/Valence 1899-1920) Includes brief histories, lists of officers, and documents for the monasteries in each diocese of France.

408
Beaunier, Dom *Recueil historique, chronologique, et topographique des archevechez, evêchez, abbayes et prieurez de France* 2 vols (Paris 1726); new ed by Jean-Martial Besse et al, *Abbayes et prieurés de l'ancienne France* (Archives 1, 4, 7, 10, 12, 14, 15, 17, 19, 36, 37, 45; Paris/Ligugé - Paris 1905ff)
The following volumes of the new edition have appeared: Introduction, I (Paris), II (Aix, Arles, Avignon, Embrun), III (Auch, Bordeaux), IV (Albi, Narbonne, Toulouse), V (Bourges), VI (Sens), VII (Rouen), VIII (Tours), IX (Vienne), X and XII (Lyon). XIV (Arras) is in course of publication by Jean Becquet in *Rev Mab* nos 241, 243, 245, and 247 (1970-2).

409
Trévillers, Jules de *Sequania monastica. Dictionnaire des abbayes, prieurés, couvents, collèges et hôpitaux conventuels, ermitages de Franche-Comté et du diocèse de Besançon antérieurs à 1790* (Vesoul [1949]) and *Sequania monastica ...: Premier supplément suivi de notes pour servir à l'histoire de l'érémitisme en Franche-Comté* (Vesoul [1955]).

410
Poirier-Coutansais, Françoise *Les abbayes bénédictines du diocèse de Reims* (Gallia monastica, ed Jean-François Lemarignier, 1; Paris 1974)
On this project, see *Rev d'hist ecc* 56 (1961) 793-812.

General

411
Voyage littéraire de deux religieux bénédictins de la congrégation de Saint Maur 2 vols (Paris 1717-24)
This account of the travels of Edmond Martène (**744, 824**) and Ursin Durand in search of medieval monastic texts contains much historical and archaeological material.
412
Ambroise, Georges *Les moines du moyen âge. Leur influence intellectuelle et politique en France* (1942) 2nd ed (Paris 1946).

Early and High Middle Ages

413
Besse, Jean-Martial *Les moines de l'ancienne France. Période gallo-romaine et mérovingienne* (Archives 2; Paris 1906).
414
Sulpicius Severus *Vie de Saint Martin* ed and trans Jacques Fontaine. 3 vols (Sources chrétiennes 133-135: Série des textes monastiques d'Occident 22-24; Paris 1967-9)
Vols II-III contain notes and commentary.
415
Saint Martin et son temps. Mémorial du XVIe centenaire des débuts du monachisme en Gaule, 361-1961 (Stud Ans 46; Rome 1961)
See **103, 168, 507**.
416
Mémorial de l'année martinienne M.DCCCC.LX-M.DCCCC.LXI. Seizième centenaire de l'abbaye de Ligugé. Centenaire de la découverte du tombeau de Saint Martin à Tours (Bibliothèque de la Société d'histoire ecclésiastique de la France = *Revue d'histoire de l'église de France* 47 [1961]; Paris 1962)
See **879**.
417
Luff, Stanley G. A. 'A Survey of Primitive Monasticism in Central Gaul (c. 350 to 700)' *Downside Review* 70 (1952) 180-203.
418
Courtois, Christian 'L'évolution du monachisme en Gaule de St Martin à St Colomban' *Monachesimo* **161**, 47-72.

419
O'Sullivan, Jeremiah F. 'Early Monasticism in Gaul' *American Benedictine Review* 16 (1965) 32-46.

420
Ueding, Leo *Geschichte des Klostergründungen der frühen Merowingerzeit* (Historische Studien, ed Ebering, 261; Berlin 1935).

421
Laporte, Jean 'Les monastères francs et l'avènement des Pippinnides' *Rev Mab* 30 (1940) 1-30.

422
Lemarignier, Jean-François 'Structures monastiques et structures politiques dans la France de la fin du Xe et des débuts du XIe siècle' *Monachesimo* **161**, 357-400; revised Eng trans in *Lordship and Community in Medieval Europe* ed Frederic L. Cheyette (New York 1968) 100-27.

Regions

423
Burg, André Marcel 'Les débuts du monachisme en Alsace. Hypothèses et vraisemblances' *Archives de l'église d'Alsace* 23 (NS, 7; 1956) 23-36.

424
Dubois, Jacques 'L'implantation monastique dans le Bugey au moyen âge' *Journal des savants* 1971, 15-31; and 'Moines et monastères du Bugey' *Le Bugey* 49 (1962) 1-63.

425
Hourlier, Jacques 'L'implantation monastique dans la Champagne du Nord' *Mémoires de la Société d'agriculture, commerce, sciences et arts du département de la Marne* 86 (1971) 49-78.

426
Laporte, Jean 'Les origines du monachisme dans la province de Rouen' *Rev Mab* 31 (1941) 1-13, 25-41, 49-68.

427
[Poirier-]Coutansais, Françoise 'Les monastères du Poitou avant l'an mil' *Rev Mab* 53 (1963) 1-21.

428
Oury, Guy M. 'Recherches sur les anciens monastères de la Touraine méridionale' *Rev Mab* 55 (1965) 97-119.

429

Guillot, Olivier *Le comte d'Anjou et son entourage au XIe siècle* 2 vols
(Paris 1972)
I, 127-93, on monasteries.

430

Bligny, Bernard *L'église et les ordres religieux dans le royaume de Bourgogne aux XIe et XIIe siècles* (Collection des cahiers d'histoire publiée par
les universités de Clermont, Lyon, Grenoble 4; Paris 1960).

431

*La Normandie bénédictine au temps de Guillaume le Conquérant (XIe
siècle)* (Lille 1967)
32 articles mostly on individual monasteries.

432

Matthew, Donald J. A. *The Norman Monasteries and their English
Possessions* (Oxford Historical Series; Oxford 1962).

433

Bruhat, L. *Le monachisme en Saintonge et en Aunis (XIe et XIIe siècles).
Etude administrative et économique* (La Rochelle 1907).

Late Middle Ages

434

Denifle, Henri *La désolation des églises, monastères et hôpitaux en France
pendant la guerre de cent ans* 2 vols in 3 (Paris 1897-9).

435

Clergeac, Adrien 'La désolation des églises, monastères et hôpitaux de
Gascogne (1356-1378)' *Revue de Gascogne* NS, 5 (1905) 289-317; and
'Les abbayes de Gascogne du XIIe siècle au Grand Schisme d'Occident' *ibid*
NS, 6 (1906) 316-29, 529-44; NS, 7 (1907) 15-29.

Canons

436

Griffe, Elie 'La réforme canoniale en pays audois aux XIe et XIIe siècles'
Bulletin de littérature ecclésiastique 44 (1943) 76-92, 137-49.

437

Becquet, Jean 'Les chanoines réguliers en Limousin aux XIe et XIIe siècles'
Anal praem 36 (1960) 193-235.

438
Parisse, Michel 'Les chanoines réguliers en Lorraine. Fondations, expansion (XIe-XIIe siècles)' *Annales de l'Est* 5 S, 20 (1968) 347-88.

HOLY ROMAN EMPIRE (GERMANY AND AUSTRIA)

Cf 3, 193, 195, 269, 282-5, 299, 310-11, 340, 344, 346, 352, 404, 406, 574, 581-2, 602, 612-13, 616, 626-8, 635-6, 646-50, 654, 684, 692, 729-33, 786, 819, 899, 929-30, 950-2, 1025.

Repertories

439
Stengel, Carl *Monasteriologia: in quam insignium aliquot monasteriorum familiae s. Benedicti in Germaniam, origines, fundatores, clarique viri ex eis oriundi describuntur* 2 vols (Augsburg 1619-38)
In the title to vol II, *Austriam et* is added before *Germaniam*. Includes brief accounts, with engravings, of 35 monasteries.

440
Brunner, Sebastian *Ein Benediktinerbuch. Geschichte und Beschreibung der bestehenden und Anführung der aufgehobenen Benediktiner-stifte in Österreich-Ungarn, Deutschland und der Schweiz* (Würzburg 1880)
Cf the two parallel volumes, with contributions by various authors, for houses of Cistercians and canons (Würzburg 1881-3).

441
Germania sacra. Historisch-statistische Darstellung der deutschen Bistümer, Domkapitel, Kollegiat- und Pfarrkirchen, Klöster und der sonstigen kirchlichen Institute [Alte Reihe] 5 vols (Berlin 1929ff); *Germania sacra. Historisch-statistische Beschreibung der Kirche des alten Reiches* NS, 8 vols to date (Berlin/Berlin - New York 1962ff); and *Germania sacra. Historisch-statistische Beschreibung der Kirche des alten Reiches. Die Bistümer der Kirchenprovinz Magdeburg* 1 vol in 2 paged consecutively (Berlin - New York 1972)
The exact relation between these volumes is hard to establish, but the third title appears to be a continuation of the first. Published volumes deal with the dioceses of Magdeburg, Mainz, Cologne, and Trier.

442
Lindner, Pirmin *Monasticon metropolis salzburgensis antiquae. Verzeich-*

nisse aller Aebte und Pröpste der Klöster der alten Kirchenprovinz Salzburg
(Salzburg 1908)
Comes down to modern times.

443
Hemmerle, Josef *Die Benediktiner-klöster in Bayern* (Germania benedictina 2; Augsburg 1970)
This is the first of eleven planned volumes, with alphabetical lists of abbeys and officers, bibliographies, and maps.

444
Krausen, Edgar *Die Klöster des Zisterzienserordens in Bayern* (Bayerische Heimatforschung 7; Munich - Pasing 1953).

445
Žák, Alfons *Österreichisches Klosterbuch. Statistik der Orden und Kongregationen der katholischen Kirche in Österreich* (Vienna - Leipzig 1911)
Mostly modern but with some historical material.

General Church Histories

446
Hauck, Albert *Kirchengeschichte Deutschlands* (1887-1920) 2nd-4th ed
5 vols [V in 2 parts paged consecutively] (Leipzig 1904-20).

447
Bauerreiss, Romuald *Kirchengeschichte Bayerns* 7 vols (St Ottilien [1949]-70)
Vols I-V come down through the fifteenth century.

448
Tüchle, Hermann *Kirchengeschichte Schwabens* 2 vols (Stuttgart 1950-54).

449
Schlesinger, Walter *Kirchengeschichte Sachsens im Mittelalter* 2 vols (Mitteldeutsche Forschungen 27; Cologne - Graz 1962).

General

450
Landers, Ernst *Die deutschen Klöster vom Ausgang Karls des Grossen bis zum Wormser Konkordat und ihr Verhältnis zu den Reformen* (Historische Studien, ed Ebering, 339; Berlin 1938).

451
Tomek, Ernst *Studien zur Reform der deutschen Klöster im XI. Jahrhundert*, I. *Die Frühreform* (Studien und Mitteilungen aus dem kirchengeschichtlichen Seminar der theologischen Fakultät der k. k. Universität in Wien 4; Vienna 1910) No more published; cf also his 'Die Reform der deutschen Klöster vom 10.-12. Jahrhundert' *Stud Mitt* 32 (1911) 65-84.

452
Voigt, Friedrich Otto *Die Klosterpolitik der salischen Kaiser und Könige mit besonderer Berücksichtigung Heinrichs IV. bis zum Jahre 1077* (Leipzig 1888).

453
Feierabend, Hans *Die politische Stellung der deutschen Reichsabteien während des Investiturstreites* (Historische Untersuchungen 3; Breslau 1913).

Regions

454
Störmer, Wilhelm 'Fernstrasse und Kloster. Zur Verkehrs- und Herrschaftsstruktur des westlichen Altbayern im frühen Mittelalter' *Zs für bayerische Landesgeschichte* 29 (1966) 299-343.

455
Engelmann, Johannes *Untersuchungen zur klösterlichen Verfassungsgeschichte in den Diözesen Magdeburg, Meissen, Merseburg und Zeitz-Wannburg (Etwa 950 bis etwa 1350)* (Beiträge zur mittelalterlichen und neueren Geschichte 4; Jena 1933).

456
Rosen, Reiner 'Die Stellung der kölner Erzbischöfe von Heribert bis Friedrich I. zu den Klöstern (999-1131)' *Jahrbuch des kölnischen Geschichtsvereins* 41 (1967) 119-81.

457
Büttner, Heinrich 'Das Erzstift Mainz und die Klosterreform im 11. Jahrhundert' *Archiv für mittelrheinische Kirchengeschichte* 1 (1949) 30-64.

458
Falck, Ludwig 'Klosterfreiheit und Klosterschutz. Die Klosterpolitik der mainzer Erzbischöfe von Adalbert I. bis Heinrich I. (1100-1153)' *Archiv für mittelrheinische Kirchengeschichte* 8 (1956) 21-75.

459

Jordan, Karl 'Studien zur Klosterpolitik Heinrichs des Löwen' *Archiv für Urkundenforschung* 17 (1941-2) 1-31.

460

Demm, Eberhard *Reformmönchtum und Slawenmission im 12. Jahrhundert. Wertsoziologisch-geistesgeschichtliche Untersuchungen zu den Viten Bischof Ottos von Bamberg* (Historische Studien, ed Ebering, 419; Lübeck - Hamburg 1970) Cf Jürgen Petersohn in *Deutsches Archiv* 27 (1971) 314-72.

461

Wollasch, Hans-Josef *Die Anfänge des Klosters St Georgen im Schwarzwald* (Forschungen zur oberrheinischen Landesgeschichte 14; Freiburg B. 1964).

462

Schmid, Karl *Kloster Hirsau und seine Stifter* (Forschungen zur oberrheinischen Landesgeschichte 9; Freiburg B. 1959).

463

Jakobs, Hermann *Die Hirsauer. Ihre Ausbreitung und Rechtsstellung im Zeitalter des Investiturstreites* (Kölner historische Abhandlungen 4; Cologne - Graz 1961) Cf **768**.

464

Jakobs, Hermann *Der Adel in der Klosterreform von St Blasien* (Kölner historische Abhandlungen 16; Cologne - Graz 1968).

465

Schwarzmaier, Hansmartin *Königtum, Adel und Klöster im Gebiet zwischen oberer Iller und Lech* (Veröffentlichungen der schwäbischen Forschungsgemeinschaft bei der Kommission für bayerische Landesgeschichte I, 7; Augsburg 1961).

Late Middle Ages

466

Opladen, Peter *Die Stellung der deutschen Könige zu den Orden im dreizehnten Jahrhundert* (Bonn 1908).

467

Heldwein, Johannes *Die Klöster Bayerns am Ausgange des Mittelalters* Munich 1913)

Chapters on religious life, charitable work, learning, art, and moral conditions.

468
Stifte und Klöster. Entwicklung und Bedeutung im Kulturleben Südtirols (Jahrbuch des südtiroler Kulturinstituts 2; Bolzano 1962) Innichen, Neustift, Marienberg, and other houses.

469
Zibermayr, Ignaz *Die Legation des Kardinals Nikolaus Cusanus und die Ordensreform in der Kirchenprovinz Salzburg* (Reformationsgeschichtliche Studien und Texte 29; Münster W. 1914).

470
Redlich, Virgil *Johann Rode von St Mathias bei Trier. Ein deutscher Reformabt des 15. Jahrhunderts* (Beiträge 11; Münster W. 1923).

Cistercians

471
Winter, Franz *Die Cistercienser des nordöstlichen Deutschlands. Ein Beitrag zur Kirchen- und Kulturgeschichte des deutschen Mittelalters* 3 vols (Gotha 1868-71).

472
Gottschalk, Joseph 'Die Bedeutung der Zisterzienser für die Ostsiedlung, besonders in Schlesien. Ein Literaturbericht' *Zs für Ostforschung* 15 (1966) 67-106.

473
Epperlein, Siegfried 'Gründungsmythos deutscher Zisterzienserklöster westlich und östlich der Elbe im hohen Mittelalter und der Bericht des leubuser Mönches im 14. Jahrhundert' *Jahrbuch für Wirtschaftsgeschichte* 1967.3, 303-35
Argues Cistercian foundations were part of German colonisation in East.

Canons

Cf **558**.

474
Winter, Franz *Die Prämonstratenser des zwölften Jahrhunderts und ihre Bedeutung für das nordöstliche Deutschland. Ein Beitrag zur Geschichte der Christianisirung und Germanisirung des Wendenlandes* (Berlin 1865).

475

Deckers, Hans Laurenz 'Die geschichtliche Bedeutung der Prämonstratenser mit besonderer Berücksichtigung ihrer mittelalterlichen Niederlassungen im Rheinland' *Anal praem* 36 (1960) 247-86; 37 (1961) 31-74, 243-61.

476

Backmund, Norbert *Die Chorherrenorden und ihre Stifte in Bayern. Augustinerchorherren, Prämonstratenser, Chorherren vom hl Geist, Antoniter* (Passau 1966).

HUNGARY

Cf **440, 445.**

477

Fuxhoffer, Damien *Monasteriologiae regni Hungariae libri duo* (1803) ed Maurus Czinár. 2 vols (Budapest 1858-60)
Vol I: Benedictine houses; II: Regular canons, Cistercians, military orders, Augustinian hermits.

478

Juhász, Koloman *Die Stifte der tschanader Diözese im Mittelalter. Ein Beitrag zur Frühgeschichte und Kulturgeschichte des Banats* (Deutschtum und Ausland 8-9; Münster W. 1927).

479

Tunkl, Franz von 'Zur Geschichte der Benediktiner in Altungarn im Zeitalter der Arpaden' *Stud Mitt* 55 (1937) 305-20.

480

Békefi, Remigius 'Geschichte des Cistercienser-Ordens in Ungarn von 1142-1814' *Cistercienser-Chronik* 12 (1900) 1-14, 33-43, 65-71, 97-103, 129-34; 13 (1901) 65-71, 97-105, 129-37, 161-7
Translated from the Hungarian by Blasius Czilek.

481

Horváth, Tibor A. 'De primordiis circariae hungaricae ordinis praemonstratensis' *Anal praem* 13 (1937) 54-62.

IBERIAN PENINSULA

Repertories

Cf **488.**

482
Leão di Santo Thomaz *Benedictina lusitana* 2 vols (Coimbra 1644-51).
483
España sagrada ed Enrique Florez, Manuel Risco, et al. 56 vols to date
(Madrid 1747ff).

General

484
Pérez de Urbel, Justo *Los monjes españoles en la edad media* (1933-4)
2nd ed 2 vols (Madrid 1945).
485
David, Pierre *Etudes historiques sur la Galice et le Portugal du VIe au XIIe
siècle* (Collection portugaise publiée sous le patronage de l'Institut français
au Portugal 7; Lisbon - Paris 1947)
Includes among others an article on Gregory VII, Cluny, and Alfonso VI.
486
Cocheril, Maur *Etudes sur le monachisme en Espagne et au Portugal*
(Collection portugaise publiée sous le patronage de l'Institut français au
Portugal; Paris - Lisbon 1966)
Includes articles on Hispanic monasticism from its origins to the twelfth
century (pp 13-156) and on the Cistercians.
487
Orlandis, José *Estudios sobre instituciones monásticas medievales*
(Pamplona 1971)
See **353, 767, 782.**

Early Middle Ages

488
Linage Conde, Antonio *Los orígines del monacato benedictino en la*

península ibérica 3 vols (Fuentes y estudios di historia leonesa 9-11; Leon 1973)
Vol I: Pre-Benedictine Hispanic monasticism; II: Spread of *Regula Benedicti*; III: 'Monasticon hispanum'.
489
Porter, William S. 'Early Spanish Monasticism' *Laudate* 10 (1932) 2-15, 66-79, 156-67; 11 (1933) 199-207; 12 (1934) 31-52
There is a slightly revised Spanish translation of the last two parts by José Vives under the title 'Monasticismo español primitivo. El oficio monástico' *Hispania sacra* 6 (1953) 3-34.
490
Mundó, Anscari 'Il monachesimo nella peninsola iberica fino al sec. VII' *Monachesimo* 161, 73-108.

Regions

491
Herwegen, Ildefons *Das Pactum des hl Fruktuosus von Braga. Ein Beitrag zur Geschichte des suevisch-westgothischen Mönchtums und seines Rechtes* (KR Abh 40; Stuttgart 1907)
Cf Charles Julian Bishko in *Classical Folia* 27 (1973) 173-85 on this and later work on Hispanic monastic pactualism.
492
Pérez de Urbel, Justo 'El monaquismo castellano en el período posterior a San Fructuoso' *Homenaje al P. Angel C. Vega OSA = La ciudad de Dios* 181.3-4 (1968) 882-910.
493
Bishko, Charles Julian 'Salvus of Albelda and Frontier Monasticism in Tenth-Century Navarre' *Speculum* 23 (1948) 559-90.
494
Bishko, Charles Julian 'Fernando I y los orígenes de la alianza castellano leonesa con Cluny' *Cuadernos de historia de España* 47-48 (1968) 31-135; 49-50 (1969) 50-116.
495
Mattoso, José *Le monachisme ibérique et Cluny. Les monastères du diocèse de Porto de l'an mille à 1200* (Université de Louvain: Recueil de travaux d'histoire et de philologie, 4 S, 39; Louvain 1968)
Deals with monasticism in Portugal until 1200 and the triumph of Benedictinism over the old Hispanic tradition.

496
Arias, Maximino 'Los monasterios de Benedictinos de Galicia. Status quaestionis' *Stud mon* 8 (1966) 35-69.

497
Defourneaux, Marcellin *Les français en Espagne aux XIe et XIIe siècles* (Paris 1949)
Pp 17-58 on Cluniacs and Cistercians in Spain.

498
Vincke, Johannes 'Kloster und Grenzpolitik in Katalonien-Aragon während des Mittelalters' *Gesammelte Aufsätze zur Kulturgeschichte Spaniens* 3 (1931) 141-64.

Congregations

499
Hofmeister, Philipp 'Die Verfassung der ehemaligen claustralen Benediktinerkongregation in Katalonien und Aragon' *Stud Mitt* 70 (1959) 206-35.

500
Bauer, Johannes Josef 'Rechtsverhältnisse der katalanischen Klöster in ihren Klosterverbänden (9.-12. Jahrhundert)' *Gesammelte Aufsätze zur Kulturgeschichte Spaniens* 23 (1967) 1-130.

501
Colombás, García M. and Mateo M. Gost *Estudios sobre el primer siglo de San Benito de Valladolid* (Scripta et documenta 3; Montserrat 1955).

Canons

502
Bauer, Johannes Josef 'Die "vita canonica" der katalanischen Kathedralkapitel vom 9. bis zum 11. Jahrhundert' *Homenaje a Johannes Vincke para el 11 mayo 1962* (Madrid 1962-3) I, 81-112.

ITALY

Cf 264-5, 275-81, 330, 337, 612, 653, 664, 734-5, 828, 871, 931, 934.

Maps

503
Cacciamani, Giuseppe M. *Atlante storico-geografico dei Benedettini d'Italia* (Rome 1967)
15 outline maps, with lists of houses by province and congregation.

Repertories

Cf **520**.

504
Schuster, Alfredo Ildefonso *Monasticon. Elenco degli antichi monasteri benedettini nell'archidiocesi milanese* (Viboldone 1946).
505
Bedini, Balduino Gustavo *Breve prospetto delle abazie cistercensi d'Italia dalla fondazione di Cîteaux (1098) alla metà del secolo decimoquarto* (Casamari 1964)
Brief accounts of 88 abbeys.

General and Early Middle Ages

506
L'Italia benedettina ed Placido M. Lugano (Rome 1929)
Includes chapters by various authors on Montecassino, Subiaco, Cava, Camaldoli, Vallombrosa, Montevergine, Montefano, the Cistercians, Montoliveto, and San Lazzaro at Venice.
507
Penco, Gregorio *Storia del monachesimo in Italia dalle origini alla fine del medio evo* (Rome 1961)
Cf also his 'La vita monastica in Italia all'epoca di S Martino di Tours' *St Martin* **415**, 67-83; and his chapter in *Nuove questioni di storia medioevale* (Milan 1964) 701-28.

508
Spreitzenhofer, Ernest *Die Entwicklung des alten Mönchthums in Italien von seinen ersten Anfängen bis zum Auftreten des heil. Benedict* (Vienna 1894).

509
Leccisotti, Tommaso 'Le conseguenze dell'invasione longobarda per l'antico monachesimo italico (Osservazioni e critiche a proposito di alcune moderne conclusioni storiche)' *Atti del 1° Congresso internazionale di studi longobardi, Spoleto, 27-30 settembre 1951* (Centro italiano di studi sull'alto medioevo; Spoleto 1952) 369-76
Cf also his article in *Monachesimo* 161, 311-37.

510
Voigt, Karl *Die königlichen Eigenklöster im Langobardenreiche* (Gotha 1909)
Mostly on seventh and eighth centuries.

511
Grasshoff, Hans *Langobardisch-fränkisches Klosterwesen in Italien* (Göttingen 1907)
The only published portion, covering seventh to tenth centuries, of his thesis on *Das Mönchtum in Italien bis zum Zeitalter der grossen Kirchenreform.*

Regional Origins

512
Penco, Gregorio 'Le origini del monachesimo in Liguria' *Benedictina* 9 (1955) 15-30
Covers fourth to eighth centuries.

513
Penco, Gregorio 'Il monachesimo in Umbria dalle origini al sec. VII incluso' *Ricerche sull'Umbria tardo-antica e preromanica. Atti del II Convegno di studi umbri, Gubbio, 24-28 maggio 1964* (Perugia 1965) 257-76.

514
Rivera, Cesare 'Per la storia dei precursori di san Benedetto nella provincia Valeria' *Bullettino dell'Istituto storico italiano per il medio evo* 47 (1932) 25-49.

Rome

515

Gordini, Gian Domenico 'Origine e sviluppo del monachesimo a Roma'
Gregorianum 37 (1956) 220-60
Fourth to fifth centuries, including Jerome.

516

Ferrari, Guy *Early Roman Monasteries: Notes for the History of the Monasteries and Convents at Rome from the V through the X Century* (Studi di Antichità cristiana 23; Vatican City 1957).

517

Hamilton, Bernard 'The Monastic Revival in Tenth Century Rome' *Stud mon* 4 (1962) 35-68; and 'The Monastery of S Alessio and the Religious and Intellectual Renaissance in Tenth-Century Rome' *Studies in Medieval and Renaissance History* 2 (1965) 263-310
Cf **337**.

North Italy

518

Grossi, Paolo *Le abbazie benedettine nell'alto medioevo italiano. Struttura giuridica, amministrazione e giurisdizione* (Pubblicazioni della Università degli studi di Firenze: Facoltà di giurisprudenza, NS, 1; Florence 1957).

519

Bognetti, Gian Piero and Carlo Marcora *L'abbazia benedettina di Civate* (Civate 1957)
Deals with late antique and early medieval monasticism.

520

Monasteri in alta Italia dopo le invasioni saracene e magiare (sec. X-XII) (Relazioni e comunicazioni presentate al XXXII Congresso storico subalpino: III Convegno di storia della chiesa in Italia [Pinerolo 6-9 settembre 1964]; Turin 1966)
Includes articles on the Cistercians (Raoul Manselli), Carthusians (Bernard Bligny), regular canons (Cosimo Damiano Fonseca), and on many individual houses; also a repertory of monasteries in North Italy (pp 633-785) and a bibliography.

521

Perret, André 'Les origines de l'expansion monastique en Savoie'

Mémoires de l'Académie des sciences, belles-lettres et arts de Savoie 6 S, 1 (1953) 29-59
Studies black Benedictines and reformed orders.

522
Zerbi, Piero 'Monasteri e riforma a Milano (dalla fine del secolo X agli inizi del XII)' *Aevum* 24 (1950) 44-60, 166-78.

523
Miccoli, Giovanni 'Aspetti del monachesimo toscano nel secolo XI' *Chiesa gregoriana. Ricerche sulla riforma del secolo XI* (Storici antichi e moderni, NS, 17; Florence 1966) 47-73.

524
Sambin, Paolo *Ricerche di storia monastica medioevale* (Miscellanea erudita 9; Padua 1959)
Monasteries in and near Padua in thirteenth to fifteenth centuries.

Greek Monasticism in Central and South Italy and Sicily

Cf **44**.

525
Scaduto, Mario *Il monachismo basiliano nella Sicilia medievale. Rinascita e decadenza, sec. XI-XIV* (Storia e letteratura 18; Rome 1947).

526
Michel, Anton 'Die griechischen Klostersiedlungen zu Rom bis zur Mitte des 11. Jahrhunderts' *Ostkirchliche Studien* 1 (1952) 32-45.

527
Ménager, Léon-Robert 'La "byzantinisation" religieuse de l'Italie méridionale (IXe-XIIe siècles) et la politique monastique des Normands d'Italie' *Rev d'hist ecc* 53 (1958) 747-74; 54 (1959) 5-40.

528
Borsari, Silvano *Il monachesimo bizantino nella Sicilia e nell'Italia meridionale prenormanne* (Istituto italiano per gli studi storici in Napoli 14; Naples 1963)
Cf also his 'Monasteri bizantini nell'Italia meridionale longobarda (sec. X e XI)' *Archivio storico per le province napoletane* 71 (NS, 32; 1950-1) 1-16.

529
Guillou, André 'Grecs d'Italie du sud et de Sicile au moyen âge. Les moines' *Ecole française de Rome: Mélanges d'archéologie et d'histoire* 75 (1963)

79-110
Revised translation of article in *Eremitismo* **304**, 355-79, with map.

530
Cappelli, Biagio *Il monachesimo basiliano ai confini calabro-lucani*
(Deputazione di storia patria per la Calabria: Collana storica 3; Naples 1963)
Covers tenth to fifteenth centuries.

531
Patlagean, Evelyne 'Recherches récentes et perspectives sur l'histoire du monachisme italo-grec' *Rivista di storia della chiesa in Italia* 22 (1968) 146-66.

532
Pertusi, Agostino 'Rapporti tra il monachesimo italo-greco ed il monachesimo bizantino nell'alto medio evo' *La chiesa greca in Italia dall'VIII al XVI secolo. Atti del Convegno storico interecclesiale (Bari, 30 apr. - 4 magg. 1969)* (Italia sacra 20-22; Padua 1972-3) [II] 473-520.

Norman Kingdom

533
White, Lynn T., Jr *Latin Monasticism in Norman Sicily* (Mediaeval Academy of America: Publication 31 [Monograph 13]; Cambridge, Mass. 1938).

534
Ménager, Léon-Robert 'Les fondations monastiques de Robert Guiscard, duc de Pouille et de Calabre' *Quellen und Forschungen aus italienischen Archiven und Bibliotheken* 39 (1959) 1-116.

535
Leccisotti, Tommaso 'Ruggero II e il monachesimo benedettino' *VII Centenario della morte di Ruggero II. Atti del Convegno internazionale di studi ruggeriani (21-25 aprile 1954)* (Palermo 1955) [I], 63-72.

536
Dupré Theseider, Eugenio 'Sugli inizi dello stanziamento cisterciense nel regno di Sicilia' *Studi medievali in onore di Antonino de Stefano* (Palermo 1956) 203-18.

LOW COUNTRIES (HOLLAND AND BELGIUM)

Cf 341-2, 345, 644, 693, 701-4, 968.

Repertories

537
Monasticon belge 4 vols (Bruges/Gembloux/Liège 1890ff)
Vol I.1 (1890): Namur; I.2 (1890-7): Hainault; II (1928-9): Liège; III.1-2
(1960-6): Western Flanders; IV.1-6 (1964-73): Brabant.
538
Michel, Edouard *Abbayes et monastères de Belgique* (Brussels - Paris
1923)
Brief accounts, with bibliographies, of 95 monasteries.
539
Schoengen, Michael *Monasticon batavum* 3 vols and suppl (Verhandelingen
der Nederlandsche Akademie van Wetenschappen, Afdeeling Letterkunde,
NS, 45; Amsterdam 1941-2)
Vol I: Franciscans; II: Augustinians; III: Benedictines.

General

540
Berlière, Ursmer 'Coup d'oeil historique sur l'ordre bénédictin en Belgique
dans le passé et dans le présent' *Mélanges publiés par les abbayes bénédictines de la congrégation belge à l'occasion du XIVe centenaire de la fondation du Mont-Cassin, 529-1929 = Revue liturgique et monastique* 7-8
(Maredsous - Louvain - St-André-lez-Bruges 1929) 158-242
Includes a list of monasteries and map. Title reads both 'bénédictin' and
'de S Benoît'.
541
Moreau, Edouard de *Les abbayes de Belgique (VIIe-XIIe siècles)* (Brussels
1952)
Cf also the relevant parts of his *Histoire de l'église en Belgique* 5 vols and
complementary vol of maps. 2nd ed of I-II (Museum lessianum: Section
historique 1-3, 11-12, 15; Brussels [1946]-52).

542
Hodüm, Arthur 'La réforme monastique d'Arnoul le Grand, comte de Flandre' *Bulletin trimestriel de la Société académique des antiquaires de la Morinie* 18 (1957) 577-603
Translation of Dutch version published in 1945.

543
Canivez, Joseph-Marie *L'ordre de Cîteaux en Belgique des origines (1132) au XXme siècle. Aperçu d'histoire monastique* (Forges lez-Chimay 1926).

544
Dereine, Charles *Les chanoines réguliers au diocèse de Liège avant Saint Norbert* (Académie royale de Belgique: Classe des lettres et des sciences morales et politiques, Mémoires in -8°, 2 S, 47.1; Brussels 1952)
Cf Hubert Silvestre in *Revue belge de philologie et d'histoire* 31 (1953) 65-74.

545
Haenens, Albert d' *L'abbaye Saint-Martin de Tournai de 1290 à 1350. Origines, évolution et dénouement d'une crise* (Université de Louvain: Recueil de travaux d'histoire et de philologie, 4 S, 23; Louvain 1961).

POLAND

546
Albers, Bruno 'Zur Geschichte des Benedictiner-Ordens in Polen' *Stud Mitt* 15 (1894) 194-232.

547
David, Pierre *Les bénédictins et l'ordre de Cluny dans la Pologne médiévale* (Publications du Centre franco-polonais de recherches historiques de Cracovie I, 1; Paris 1939)
Cf his 'Le monachisme bénédictin et l'ordre de Cluny dans la Pologne médiévale' *Rev Mab* 27 (1937) 43-54, 125-38, 157-87; 28 (1938) 10-14, 70-83.

548
Kłoczowski, Jerzy 'La vie monastique en Pologne et en Bohême aux XI-XII siècles (jusqu'à la moitié du XII siècle)' *Monachesimo* **221**, 153-69.

549
Kłoczowski, Jerzy 'Les Cisterciens en Pologne, du XIIe au XIIIe siècle' *Cîteaux* 21 (1970) 111-34
Revised translation of Polish version published in 1968.

SCANDINAVIA

Cf 333-4.

550
Oppermann, Charles J. A. *The English Missionaries in Sweden and Finland* (London 1937)
Goes to the thirteenth century, with a chapter on 'The Coming of the Monks'.

551
France, C. A. J. 'English Influence on Danish Monasticism' *Downside Review* 78 (1960) 181-91.

552
King, Peter 'The Cathedral Priory of Odense in the Middle Ages' *Kirkehistoriske Samlinger* 7 S, 6 (1966) 1-20.

553
Nyberg, Tore 'Lists of Monasteries in Some Thirteenth-Century Wills. Monastic History and Historical Method: a Contribution' *Mediaeval Scandinavia* 5 (1972) 49-74.

554
McGuire, Brian P. 'Property and Politics at Esrum Abbey, 1151-1251' *Mediaeval Scandinavia* 6 (1973) 122-50.

SWITZERLAND

Cf 440, 906, 920-2.

555
Henggeler, Rudolf *Monasticon-benedictinum Helvetiae* 4 vols to date (Zug 1931ff)
Profession books of Swiss Benedictine monasteries.

556
Festgabe Hans Nabholz zum siebzigsten Geburtstag (Aarau 1944)
Includes articles on nunneries in the diocese of Chur and on Wagenhausen, Einsiedeln, and Muri.

557
Egger, Bonaventura *Geschichte der Cluniazenser-Klöster in der Westschweiz bis zum Auftreten der Cisterzienser* (Freiburger historische Studien 3; Freiburg S. 1907).

558

Siegwart, Josef *Die Chorherren- und Chorfrauengemeinschaften in der deutschsprachigen Schweiz vom 6. Jahrhundert bis 1160 mit einem Überblick über die deutsche Kanonikerreform des 10. und 11. Jh.* (Freiburg S. 1962).

MEDIEVAL MONASTICISM

PART III: MONASTIC LIFE AND INSTITUTIONS

General Considerations

FOUNDATION

566
Reicke, Siegfried 'Zum Rechtsvorgang der Klosterverlegung im Mittelalter' *Festschrift Ulrich Stutz zum siebzigsten Geburtstag* (KR Abh 117-18; Stuttgart 1938) 53-119.

567
Galbraith, Vivian H. 'Monastic Foundation Charters of the Eleventh and Twelfth Centuries' *Cambridge Historical Journal* 4.3 (1934) 205-22, 296-8.

SITES AND NAMES OF MONASTERIES

Cf **424-5, 451, 908-9.**

568
Gougaud, Louis 'Les sites et les noms des moutiers de France' *Coutumes* **813**, 1-13.

569
Plandé, Romain 'Géographie et monachisme. Sites et importance géographique de quelques abbayes de la région de l'Aude' *Mélanges Albert Dufourcq* (Paris [1932]) 21-35.

570
Donkin, Robert A. 'The Site Changes of Mediaeval Cistercian Monasteries' *Geography* 44 (1959) 251-8.

571
Dimier, Marie-Anselme 'Les emplacements des monastères cisterciens' *Bulletin de la Société nationale des antiquaires de France* 1943-4, 231-8; and 'Cîteaux et les emplacements malsains' *Cîteaux* 6 (1955) 89-97.

572
Laurent, Jacques 'Les noms des monastères cisterciens dans la toponomie européenne' *Bernard et son temps* **256**, I, 168-204.

573
Dimier, Marie-Anselme *Clarté paix et joie. Les beaux noms des monastères de Cîteaux en France* (La Clarté-Dieu 15; Lyon 1944).

574
Zimmermann, Gerd 'Patrozinienwahl und Frömmigkeitswandel im Mittelalter dargestellt an Beispielen aus dem alten Bistum Würzburg' *Würzburger Diözesangeschichtsblätter* 20 (1958) 24-126; 21 (1959) 5-124
On the patron saints of monastic and other churches.

NUMBERS OF MONKS

Cf Janin **81**, 29-31 for Byzantium.

575
Guillemain, Bernard 'Chiffres et statistiques pour l'histoire ecclésiastique du moyen âge' *Le Moyen Âge* 59 (4 S, 8; 1953) 341-65.

576
Berlière, Ursmer 'Le nombre des moines dans les anciens monastères' *Rev bén* 41 (1929) 231-61; 42 (1930) 19-42.

577
Russell, Josiah C. 'The Clerical Population of Medieval England' *Traditio* 2 (1944) 177-212
Cf Knowles **369**, 359-65 and Moorman **380**, 402-12.

578
Dubois, Jacques 'Du nombre des moines dans les monastères' *Lettre de Ligugé* 1969.2 (no 134) 24-36
From seventh to twentieth century.

SOCIAL ORIGINS OF MONKS

579
Penco, Gregorio 'La composizione sociale delle communità monastiche nei primi secoli' *Stud mon* 4 (1962) 257-81.

580
Berlière, Ursmer *Le recrutement dans les monastères bénédictins aux XIII*[e] *et XIV*[e] *siècles* (Académie royale de Belgique: Classe des lettres et des sciences morales et politiques, Mémoires in -8° [2 S] 18.6; Brussels 1924).

581
Schulte, Aloys *Der Adel und die deutsche Kirche im Mittelalter. Studien zur Sozial-, Rechts- und Kirchengeschichte* (KR Abh 63-64; Stuttgart 1910; repr with *Nachtrag* 1922)
Deals with both secular and regular clergy.

582
Schreiner, Klaus *Sozial- und standesgeschichtliche Untersuchungen zu den Benediktinerkonventen im östlichen Schwarzwald* (Veröffentlichungen der Kommission für geschichtliche Landeskunde in Baden-Württemberg B, 31; Stuttgart 1964).

Monastic Government

Cf **142-3, 165, 167, 244, 379, 499-501, 812.**

GENERAL

583
Gasquet, Francis Aidan 'A Sketch of Monastic Constitutional History' intro to Charles de Montalembert *The Monks of the West from St Benedict to St Bernard* 6 vols (London - New York 1896) I, vii-lvi (**148**), repr in *Monastic Life* **133**, 197-242
According to Knowles, *Historian* **136**, 252 and 309, this essay was largely written by Edmund Bishop and Elphege Cody.

584
Moulin, Léo *Les formes du gouvernement local et provincial dans les ordres religieux* (Offprint from *Revue internationale des sciences administratives* nos 1, 3, 4; Brussels 1956).

585
Le Bras, Gabriel *Institutions ecclésiastiques de la chrétienté médiévale* 2 vols paged consecutively (*Histoire de l'église* **47**, XII.1-2; Paris 1959-64) Especially pp 443-525 on regular clergy.

586
Knowles, David *From Pachomius to Ignatius: A Study of the Constitutional History of the Religious Orders* (Sarum Lectures 1964-5; Oxford 1966).

CHAPTER-GENERAL

Cf 378.

587
Berlière, Ursmer 'Les chapitres généraux de l'ordre de S Benoît avant le
IVe concile de Latran (1215)' *Rev bén* 8 (1891) 255-64; 'Les chapitres
généraux de l'ordre de Saint Benoît du XIIIe au XVe siècle' *ibid* 9 (1892)
545-57; 'Les chapitres généraux de l'ordre de S Benoît' *ibid* 18 (1901)
364-98; 19 (1902) 38-75, 268-78, 374-411; 'Notes supplémentaires' *ibid*
22 (1905) 377-97
Partly reprinted in *Mélanges* **130**, IV, 52-171.

588
Hourlier, Jacques *Le chapitre général jusqu'au moment du Grand Schisme.
Origines - développement - étude juridique* (Paris 1936).

589
Sayers, Jane 'The Judicial Activities of the General Chapters' *Journal of
Ecclesiastical History* 15 (1964) 18-32, 168-85.

ABBOT AND COMMUNITY

590
Vogüé, Adalbert de *La communauté et l'abbé dans la règle de Saint Benoît*
(Paris 1961)
Cf Olivier Rousseau in *La vie spirituelle: Supplément* 15 (1962) 471-9.

591
Jassmeier, Joachim *Das Mitbestimmungsrecht der Untergebenen in den
älteren Männerordensverbänden* (Münchener theologische Studien,
Kanonistische Abt. 5; Munich 1954)
Pp 5-147 on orders with independent houses, mostly modern.

592
Hilpisch, Stephanus 'Der Rat der Brüder in den Benediktinerklöstern des
Mittelalters' *Stud Mitt* 67 (1956) 221-36.

ABBOT

593
Tamburini, Ascanio *De jure abbatum et aliorum praelatorum, tam*

regularium, quam saecularium episcopis inferiorum 2 vols (Rome 1629-30) Cf **314**.

594

Chamard, François 'Les abbés au moyen âge' *Revue des questions historiques* 38 (1885) 71-108.

595

Kindt, Gerard *De potestate dominativa in religione* (Universitas catholica lovaniensis: Dissertationes ad gradum magistri in facultate theologica vel in facultate iuris canonici consequendum conscriptae, 2 S, 34; Bruges - Paris - Rome 1945)

Pp 3-116 on twelfth to fifteenth centuries.

596

Salmon, Pierre *L'abbé dans la tradition monastique. Contribution à l'histoire du caractère perpétuel des supérieurs religieux en Occident* (Histoire et sociologie de l'église 2; Paris 1962; Eng trans by Claire Lavoie 1972)

Cf Armand Veilleux in *La vie spirituelle: Supplément* 21 (1968) 351-93 on this and other recent works on the position of the abbot, most of which, though historical in character, have a basically modern concern.

597

Penco, Gregorio 'La figura dell'abate nella tradizione spirituale del monachesimo' *Benedictina* 17 (1970) 1-12

Comes down through twelfth century.

Election

598

Berlière, Ursmer *Les élections abbatiales au moyen âge* (Académie royale de Belgique: Classe des lettres et des sciences morales et politiques, Mémoires in -8° [2 S] 20.3; Brussels 1927).

599

Moulin, Léo 'Sanior et maior pars. Note sur l'évolution des techniques électorales dans les ordres religieux du VIe au XIIIe siècle' *Revue historique de droit français et étranger* 4 S, 36 (1958) 368-97, 491-529.

600

Grundmann, Herbert 'Pars quamvis parva. Zur Abtwahl nach Benedikts Regel' *Festschrift Percy Ernst Schramm* (Wiesbaden 1964) I, 237-51.

601

Hallinger, Kassius 'Das Wahlrecht der Benediktusregula' *Zs für KG* 76 (1965) 233-45
Cf Herbert Grundmann *ibid* 77 (1966) 217-23.

Special Periods and Regions

602

Polzin, Johannes *Die Abtswahlen in den Reichsabteien von 1024-1056* (Greifswald 1908).

603

Lévy-Bruhl, Henri *Etude sur les élections abbatiales en France jusqu'à la fin du règne de Charles le Chauve* (Paris 1913)
Also published as vol I of his *Les élections abbatiales en France.*

604

Muller, Jean-Pierre 'Les élections abbatiales chez les Bénédictins sous Clément V (1305-1314)' *Studia benedictina* **156**, 341-65.

605

Baunach, Wolfgang 'Die Abtwahl in den Königsklöstern der spanischen Mark. Ein Beitrag zum Verhältnis von Staat und Kirche in der Karolinger-zeit' *Gesammelte Aufsätze zur Kulturgeschichte Spaniens* 19 (1962) 25-98.

606

Bauer, Johannes Josef 'Die Abtwahlen in Katalonien und Aragon während des 13. Jahrhunderts' *Römische Quartalschrift für christliche Altertums-kunde und Kirchengeschichte* 62 (1967) 18-35; and 'Die Abtwahl in Katalonien und Aragon zur Zeit des Avignoneser Papsttums' *ibid* 184-213.

Consecration

607

Hilpisch, Stephanus 'Entwicklung des Ritus des Abtsweihe in der latein-ischen Kirche' *Stud Mitt* 61 (1947-8) 53-72.

Insignia

608

Hofmeister, Philipp *Mitra und Stab der wirklichen Prälaten ohne bischöf-lichen Charakter* (KR Abh 104; Stuttgart 1928).

609
Salmon, Pierre *Etude sur les insignes du pontife dans le rit roman. Histoire et liturgie* (Rome 1955).

610
Bauerreiss, Romuald 'Abtsstab und Bischofsstab' *Stud Mitt* 68 (1957) 215-26.

Resignation

611
Noschitzka, Canisius L. 'Die kirchenrechtliche Stellung des resignierten Regularabtes unter besonderer Berücksichtigung der geschichtlichen Entwicklung im Zisterzienserorden' *Anal cist* 13 (1957) 149-314.

Relations with Outside Authorities

Cf 209, 246, 469, 604.

612

Italia pontificia ed Paul F. Kehr et al. 9 vols to date [VI and VII in 2 parts] (Berlin 1906ff); and *Germania pontificia* ed Albert Brackmann 3 vols to date [I and II in 2 parts] (Berlin 1910ff) Includes brief histories and bibliographies of monasteries.

613

Brackmann, Albert *Die Kurie und die salzburger Kirchenprovinz* (Studien und Vorarbeiten zur Germania pontificia [612] 1; Berlin 1912).

614

Letonnelier, Gaston *L'abbaye exempte de Cluny et le Saint-Siège. Etude sur le développement de l'exemption clunisienne des origines jusqu'à la fin du XIIIe siècle* (Archives 22; Ligugé - Paris 1923).

615

Bloch, Raissa 'Die Klosterpolitik Leos IX. in Deutschland, Burgund und Italien' *Archiv für Urkundenforschung* 11 (1929-30) 176-257
Cf the series of Greifswald dissertations on the monastic policies of Gregory VII (Bernhard Messing 1907), Urban II and Pascal II (Carl Korbe 1910), Calixtus II (Gregor Ender 1913), Honorius II (Paul Adamczyk 1912), Innocent II (Georg Wieczorek 1914), and Eugene III (Wilhelm Reichert 1912).

616

Kraaz, Walter *Die päpstliche Politik in Verfassungs- und Vermögensfragen deutscher Klöster im 12. Jahrhundert* (Leipzig 1902)

Papal protection, relation to abbot and community, bishops, advocates, property, etc.

617

Schreiber, Georg *Kurie und Kloster im 12. Jahrhundert. Studien zur Privilegierung, Verfassung und besonders zum Eigenkirchenwesen der vorfranziskanischen Orden vornehmlich auf Grund der Papsturkunden von Paschalis II. bis auf Lucius III. (1099-1181)* 2 vols (KR Abh 65-68; Stuttgart 1910).

618

Berlière, Ursmer 'Innocent III et la réorganisation des monastères bénédictins' *Rev bén* 32 (1920) 22-42, 145-59.

619

Berlière, Ursmer 'Honorius III et les monastères bénédictins 1216-1227' *Revue belge de philologie et d'histoire* 2 (1923) 237-65, 461-84.

620

Fabre, Paul *Etude sur le Liber censuum de l'église romaine* (Bibliothèque des Ecoles françaises d'Athènes et de Rome 62; Paris 1892) Cf also his edition of the *Liber censuum* (Paris 1910-52).

621

Hofmeister, Philipp 'Kardinäle aus dem Ordensstande' *Stud Mitt* 72 (1961) 153-70.

Papal Protection

622

Daux, Camille 'La protection apostolique au moyen âge' *Revue des questions historiques* 72 (NS, 28; 1902) 5-60.

623

Lesne, Emile 'Nicholas I et les libertés des monastères des Gaules' *Le Moyen Âge* 24 (2 S, 15; 1911) 277-306, 333-45.

624

Hirsch, Hans 'Untersuchungen zur Geschichte des päpstlichen Schutzes' *Mitteilungen des österreichischen Instituts für Geschichtsforschung* 54 (1941-2) 363-433

The last (posthumous) of Hirsch's many works on this subject; cf **134**.

625

Appelt, Heinrich 'Die Anfänge des päpstlichen Schutzes' *Mitteilungen des Instituts für österreichische Geschichtsforschung* 62 (1954) 101-11.

BISHOPS

Cf 368, 456-8.

626
Tellenbach, Gerd *Die bischöflich passauischen Eigenklöster und ihre Vogteien* (Historische Studien, ed Ebering, 173; Berlin 1928).

627
Mitterer, Sigisbert *Die bischöflichen Eigenklöster in den vom hl Bonifazius 739 gegründeten bayerischen Diözesen* (*Stud Mitt: Ergänzungsheft* 2; Munich 1929)
Salzburg, Freising, Regensburg, Passau.

Exemption

628
Goetting, Hans 'Die klösterliche Exemtion in Nord- und Mitteldeutschland vom 8. bis zum 15. Jh.' *Archiv für Urkundenforschung* 14 (1936) 105-87.

629
Lemarignier, Jean-François *Etude sur les privilèges d'exemption et de jurisdiction ecclésiastique des abbayes normandes depuis les origines jusqu' en 1140* (Archives 44; Paris 1937).

630
Lemarignier, Jean-François 'L'exemption monastique et les origines de la réforme grégorienne' *À Cluny* 206, 288-340.

631
Szaivert, Willy 'Die Entstehung und Entwicklung der Klosterexemtion bis zum Ausgang des 11. Jahrhunderts' *Mitteilungen des Instituts für österreichische Geschichtsforschung* 59 (1951) 265-98.

632
Hofmeister, Philipp 'Die Exemtion der Ordensleute vom Pfarrverband' *Archiv für katholisches Kirchenrecht* 122 (4 S, 30; 1942-3 [1947]) 46-87, 279-95; 123 (4 S, 31; 1944-8 [1948]) 9-29
Covers medieval and modern period.

633
Muller, Léo 'La notion canonique d'abbaye *nullius*' *Revue de droit canonique* 6 (1956) 115-44
Medieval origins of a modern juridical form.

SECULAR AUTHORITIES

Cf 184-6, 382, 386, 421, 429, 452, 459, 462, 464-6, 510, 534-5.

Lay Powers over Monasteries

634
Levillain, Léon *Examen critique des chartes mérovingiennes et carolingiennes de l'abbaye de Corbie* (Mémoires et documents publiés par la Société de l'Ecole des chartes 5; Paris 1902)
On monastic privileges and documents from the seventh to tenth century; cf also his 'Note sur l'immunité mérovingienne' *Revue historique de droit français et étranger* 4 S, 6 (1927) 38-67.

635
Hirsch, Hans 'Studien über die Privilegien süddeutscher Klöster des 11. und 12. Jahrhunderts' *Mitteilungen des Instituts für österreichische Geschichtsforschung: Ergänzungsband* 7 (1904-7) 471-612.

636
Mayer, Theodor *Fürsten und Staat. Studien zur Verfassungsgeschichte des deutschen Mittelalters* (Weimar 1950)
Includes articles on advocacy, royal protection and immunity, royal monasteries, etc.

637
Semmler, Josef 'Traditio und Königsschutz' *Sav-Zs, Kan Abt* 45 (1959) 1-33.

638
Schwarz, Wilhelm 'Jurisdicio und Condicio' *Sav-Zs, Kan Abt* 45 (1959) 34-98.

Regional Studies

639
Herman, Emil 'Ricerche sulle istituzioni monastiche bizantine. Typika ktetorika, caristicari e monasteri "liberi"' *Orientalia christiana periodica* 6 (1940) 293-375.

640
Lemerle, Paul 'Un aspect du rôle des monastères à Byzance. Les monastères données à des laïcs, les Charisticaires' *Académie des inscriptions et belles-lettres: Comptes rendus* 1967, 9-28.

641
Ahrweiler, Hélène 'Charisticariat et autres formes d'attribution de
fondations pieuses aux Xe-XIe siècles' *Recueil des travaux de l'Institut
d'études byzantines* 10 (1967) 1-27.

642
Senn, Félix *L'institution des avoueries ecclésiastiques en France* (Paris
1903).

643
Morin, O. *Les avoueries ecclésiastiques en Lorraine* (Nancy 1907)
Not seen.

644
Pergameni, Charles *L'avouerie ecclésiastique belge des origines à la période
bourguignonne* (Ghent 1907).

645
Dubled, Henri 'L'avouerie des monastères en Alsace au moyen âge (VIIIe-
XIIe siècle)' *Archives de l'église d'Alsace* 26 (NS, 10; 1959) 1-88; and
'L'avouerie des monastères en Alsace au moyen âge (XIIIe-XVe siècle)' *ibid*
30 (NS, 14; 1964) 65-141.

646
Waas, Adolf *Vogtei und Bede in der deutschen Kaiserzeit* 2 vols (Arbeiten
zur deutschen Rechts- und Verfassungsgeschichte 1, 5; Berlin 1919-23).

647
Hirsch, Hans *Die hohe Gerichtsbarkeit im deutschen Mittelalter* (Reichen-
berg 1922; repr with *Nachwort* by Theodor Mayer 1958).

648
Rathgen, Georg 'Untersuchungen über die eigenkirchenrechtlichen
Elemente der Kloster- und Stiftsvogtei vornehmlich nach thüringischen
Urkunden bis zum Beginn des XIII. Jahrhunderts' *Sav-Zs, Kan Abt* 17
(1928) 1-152
Includes index of monasteries and founders.

649
Otto, Eberhard F. *Die Entwicklung der deutschen Kirchenvogtei im 10.
Jahrhundert* (Abhandlungen zur mittleren und neueren Geschichte 72;
Berlin 1933)
Deals especially with comital advocacy.

650
Klebel, Ernst 'Eigenklosterrechte und Vogteien in Bayern und Deutsch-
österreich' *Mitteilungen des österreichischen Instituts für Geschichtsforschung: Ergänzungsband* 14 (1939) 175-214.

651

Santos Díez, José Luis *La encomienda de monasterios en la Corona de Castilla. Siglos X-XV* (Cuadernos del Instituto jurídico español 14; Rome - Madrid 1961).

Immunity

Cf **634, 636, 689.**

652

Kroell, Maurice *L'immunité franque* (Paris 1910).

653

Lanzani, Anna 'Le concessioni immunitarie a favore dei monasteri pavesi nell'alto medio-evo (secoli IX-XII)' *Bollettino della Società pavese di storia patria* 10 (1910) 3-54.

654

Stengel, Edmund E. *Die Immunität in Deutschland bis zum Ende des 11. Jahrhunderts*, I: *Diplomatik der deutschen Immunitäts-Privilegien vom 9. bis zum Ende des 11. Jahrhunderts* (Innsbruck, 1910) No more published.

655

Hirsch, Hans *Die Klosterimmunität seit dem Investiturstreit* (Untersuchungen zur Verfassungsgeschichte des deutschen Reiches und der deutschen Kirche; Weimar 1913; repr with *Nachwort* by Heinrich Büttner, 1967).

Economy

Cf 167, 220, 271, 292, 332, 461, 670, 999-1004, 1005-9.

GENERAL

656
Uhlhorn, Gerhard 'Der Einfluss der wirtschaftlichen Verhältnisse auf die Entwickelung des Mönchtums im Mittelalter' *Zs für KG* 14 (1894) 347-403.

657
Salvioli, Giuseppe 'Il monachismo occidentale e la sua storia economica' *Rivista italiana di sociologia* 15 (1911) 8-35.

658
Raftis, James Ambrose 'Western Monasticism and Economic Organization' *Comparative Studies in Society and History* 3 (1961) 452-69.

Benedictine Monasticism

659
Werminghoff, Albert 'Die wirtschaftstheoretischen Anschauungen der *Regula sancti Benedicti*' *Historische Aufsätze Karl Zeumer zum sechzigsten Geburtstag als Festgabe dargebracht* (Weimar 1910) 31-50.

660
Lieblang, Alice 'Die Wirtschaftsverfassung der benediktinischen Mönchsregel im besonderen die Behandlung der Besitz- und Arbeitsverhältnisse' *Stud Mitt* 49 (1931) 413-47; 50 (1932) 109-42.

CHURCH PROPERTY

661

Stutz, Ulrich *Geschichte des kirchlichen Benefizialwesens von seinen Anfängen bis auf die Zeit Alexanders III.* I.1 (Berlin 1895; repr with a foreword and supplement by Hans Erich Feine 1961) No more published; comes down to the ninth century.

662

Lesne, Emile *Histoire de la propriété ecclésiastique en France* 6 vols [II in 3 parts] (Mémoires et travaux publiés par des professeurs des facultés catholiques de Lille 6, 19, 30, 34, 44, 46, 50, 53; Lille - Paris/Lille 1910-43) See **873, 889, 894**.

663

Thiele, Augustinus 'Studien zur Vermögensbildung und Vermögensverwertung der Kirche im Merowingerreich (6. Jh.)' *Stud Mitt* 80.3-4 (1969) 7-143.

Monastic Dependents

664

Luzzatto, Gino *I servi nelle grandi proprietà ecclesiastiche italiane dei sec. IX e X* (Pisa 1910) Bobbio, Lucca, Brescia, etc.

665

Bernard, Pierre *Etude sur les esclaves et les serfs d'église en France du VIe au XIIIe siècle* (Paris 1919) Based primarily on monastic sources.

666

Berlière, Ursmer *La familia dans les monastères bénédictins du moyen âge* (Académie royale de Belgique: Classe des lettres et des sciences morales et politiques, Mémoires in -8° [2 S] 29.2; Brussels 1931).

667

Berlière, Ursmer 'Monastères et sujets au moyen âge' *Rev bén* 43 (1931) 322-41; 44 (1932) 47-70.

Byzantine Monasticism

668
Ferradou, André *Des biens des monastères à Byzance* (Bordeaux 1896).

669
Delehaye, Hippolyte *Deux typica byzantins de l'époque des Paléologues* (Académie royale de Belgique: Classe des lettres et des sciences morales et politiques, Mémoires in -8°, 2 S, 13.4; Brussels 1921).

670
Herman, Emil 'Die Regelung der Armut in den byzantinischen Klöstern' *Orientalia christiana periodica* 7 (1941) 406-60.

671
Charanis, Peter 'The Monastic Properties and the State in the Byzantine Empire' *Dumbarton Oaks Papers* 4 (1948) 53-118.

AGRICULTURE

Cf 366.

672
Maas, Walther *Les moines-défricheurs. Etudes sur les transformations du paysage au moyen-âge aux confins de la Champagne et de la Lorraine* (Moulins 1944).

673
La bonifica benedettina (Rome [1963])
Includes a bibliography by Giovanni Baffioni on Benedictine agricultural exploitation.

CISTERCIANS

Cf 241, 554, 773-5.

674
Hoffmann, Eberhard 'Die Entwicklung der Wirtschaftsprinzipien im Cisterzienserorden während des 12. und 13. Jahrhunderts' *Historisches Jahrbuch* 31 (1910) 699-727.

675
Vignes, Bernard-Joseph-Maurice 'Les doctrines économiques et morales de

Saint Bernard sur la richesse et le travail' *Revue d'histoire économique et social* 16 (1928) 547-85.

676

Roehl, Richard 'Plan and Reality in a Medieval Monastic Economy: The Cistercians' *Studies in Medieval and Renaissance History* 9 (1972) 83-113.

GRANGES

677

Bishop, Terence A. M. 'Monastic Granges in Yorkshire' *English Historical Review* 51 (1936) 193-214.

678

Donnelly, James S. 'Changes in the Grange Economy of English and Welsh Cistercian Abbeys, 1300-1540' *Traditio* 10 (1954) 399-458.

679

Donkin, Robert A. 'The Cistercian Grange in England in the 12th and 13th Centuries, with Special Reference to Yorkshire' *Stud mon* 6 (1964) 95-144

With 3 fold-out maps.

680

Platt, Colin *The Monastic Grange in Medieval England* (London - Melbourne - Toronto 1969).

681

Fournier, Gabriel 'La création de la grange de Gergovie par les Prémontrés de Saint-André et sa transformation en seigneurie (XIIe-XVIe siècles)' *Le Moyen Âge* 56 (4 S, 5; 1950) 307-55.

682

Higounet, Charles 'Les types d'exploitations cisterciennes et prémontrées du XIIIe siècle et leur rôle dans la formation de l'habitat et des paysages ruraux' *Géographie et histoire agraires (Annales de l'Est: Mémoire* 21; Nancy 1959) 260-70 (with a discussion on 270-1).

683

Higounet, Charles *La grange de Vaulerent. Structure et exploitation d'un terroir cistercien de la plaine de France XIIe-XVe siècle* (Ecole pratique des hautes études - VIe section: Centre de recherches historiques, Les hommes et la terre 10; Paris 1965).

684

Wiswe, Hans 'Grangien niedersächsischer Zisterzienserklöster. Entstehung

und Bewirtschaftung spätmittelalterlich-frühneuzeitlicher landwirtschaft-
licher Grossbetriebe' *Braunschweigisches Jahrbuch* 34 (1953) 5-134.

ECCLESIASTICAL REVENUES

685
Constable, Giles *Monastic Tithes from their Origins to the Twelfth
Century* (Cambridge Studies in Medieval Life and Thought, NS, 10;
Cambridge 1964).

686
Constable, Giles 'Monastic Possession of Churches and "Spiritualia" in the
Age of Reform' *Monachesimo* **221**, 304-31.

FINANCIAL AND COMMERCIAL ACTIVITIES

687
Génestal, Robert *Rôle des monastères comme établissements de crédit
étudié en Normandie du XIe à la fin du XIIIe siècle* (Paris 1901).

688
Whitwell, Robert J. 'English Monasteries and the Wool Trade in the 13th
Century' *Vierteljahrschrift für Social- und Wirtschaftsgeschichte* 2 (1904)
1-33.

689
Imbart de la Tour, Pierre 'Des immunités commerciales accordées aux
églises du VIIe au IXe siècle' *Etudes d'histoire du moyen âge dédiées à
Gabriel Monod* (Paris 1896) 71-87 and in his *Questions d'histoire sociale
et religieuse. Epoque féodale* (Paris 1907) 1-29.

690
Simpson, John B. 'Coal-mining by the Monks' *Transactions of the
Institution of Mining Engineers* 39 (1909-10) 573-98
In England from the twelfth to the sixteenth century, with bibliography
and map.

691
Kalischer, Erwin *Beiträge zur Handelsgeschichte der Klöster zur Zeit der
Grossgrundherrschaften* (Berlin 1911)
Sections on regalia, monastic markets, trade, etc, down to the twelfth
century.

692
Wagner, Hermann F. 'Salz und Wein in der Klosterwirtschaft der Vorzeit'
Stud Mitt 37 (1916) 48-63
Mostly on South German monasteries.

693
Van Werveke, Hans 'Comment les établissements religieux belges se
procuraient-ils du vin au haut moyen âge?' *Revue belge de philologie et
d'histoire* 2 (1923) 643-62.

MONASTERIES AND TOWNS

694
Lestocquoy, Jean-François 'Abbayes et origines des villes' *Revue d'histoire
de l'église de France* 33 (1947) 108-12.

695
Higounet, Charles 'Cisterciens et bastides' *Le Moyen Âge* 56 (4 S, 5;
1950) 69-84
Building of bastides on Cistercian granges in thirteenth to fourteenth
centuries.

INTERNAL ECONOMY

696
Lesne, Emile 'L'économie domestique d'un monastère au IXe siècle d'après
les statuts d'Adalhard, abbé de Corbie' *Mélanges d'histoire du moyen âge
offerts à M. Ferdinand Lot* (Paris 1925) 385-420.

Mensa

697
Lesne, Emile *L'origine des menses dans le temporel des églises et des
monastères de France au IXe siècle* (Mémoires et travaux publiés par des
professeurs des facultés catholiques de Lille 7; Lille - Paris 1910).

698
John, Eric 'The Division of the Mensa in Early English Monasteries'
Journal of Ecclesiastical History 6 (1955) 143-55.

Corrodies

699

Lesne, Emile 'Une source de la fortune monastique.' Les donations à charge de pension alimentaire du VIIIe au Xe siècle' *Mélanges de philosophie et d'histoire publiés à l'occasion du cinquantenaire de la faculté des lettres de l'Université catholique de Lille* (Mémoires et travaux publiés par des professeurs des facultés catholiques de Lille 32; Lille 1927) 33-47 Such payments were not yet called corrodies but *stipendia, prebenda, provenda, victus,* and *vestitus*.

700

Stuckert, Howard M. *Corrodies in the English Monasteries. A Study in English Social History of the Middle Ages* (Philadelphia 1923).

REGIONS

Belgium

701

Hansay, Alfred *Etude sur la formation et l'organisation économique du domaine de l'abbaye de Saint-Trond* (Université de Gand: Recueil de travaux publiés par la faculté de philosophie et lettres 22; Ghent 1899).

702

Simenon, Guillaume *L'organisation économique de l'abbaye de Saint-Trond depuis la fin du XIIIe siècle jusqu'au commencement du XVIIe siècle* (Brussels 1913).

703

Genicot, Léopold 'L'évolution des dons aux abbayes dans le comté de Namur du Xe au XIVe siècle' *XXXe Congrès de la Fédération archéologique et historique de Belgique. Annales* (Brussels 1936) 133-48.

704

Genicot, Léopold 'Donations de *villae* ou défrichements. Les origines du temporel de l'abbaye de Lobbes' *Miscellanea historica in honorem Alberti de Meyer* (Université de Louvain: Recueil de travaux d'histoire et de philologie, 3 S, 22-23; Louvain - Brussels 1946) I, 286-96.

British Isles

705

Snape, Robert H. *English Monastic Finances in the Later Middle Ages* (Cambridge Studies in Medieval Life and Thought; Cambridge 1926).

706

Page, Frances M. *The Estates of Crowland Abbey: A Study in Manorial Organisation* (Cambridge Studies in Economic History; Cambridge 1934).

707

Raftis, James Ambrose *The Estates of Ramsay Abbey: A Study in Economic Growth and Organization* (Pontifical Institute of Mediaeval Studies: Studies and Texts 3; Toronto 1957).

708

Graves, Coburn V. 'The Economic Activities of the Cistercians in Medieval England (1128-1307)' *Anal cist* 13 (1957) 3-60.

709

Donkin, Robert A. 'The English Cistercians and Assarting, c.1128- c.1350' *Anal cist* 20 (1964) 49-75.

710

Donkin, Robert A. 'Settlement and Depopulation on Cistercian Estates during the Twelfth and Thirteenth Centuries, especially in Yorkshire' *Bulletin of the Institute of Historical Research* 33 (1960) 141-65 See also other works by Donkin listed in **14**.

711

Waites, Bryan *Moorland and Vale-Land Farming in North-East Yorkshire: The Monastic Contribution in the Thirteenth and Fourteenth Centuries* (University of York: Borthwick Institute of Historical Research, Borthwick Papers 32; York 1967).

712

Williams, David H. *The Welsh Cistercians: Aspects of their Economic History* (Pontypool 1969) Chapters on site changes, landed property, woods, wool, fishing, and minerals mainly from thirteenth-sixteenth centuries.

713

Kershaw, Ian *Bolton Priory: The Economy of a Northern Monastery, 1286-1325* (Oxford Historical Monographs; Oxford 1973).

France

714

Sackur, Ernst 'Beiträge zur Wirthschaftsgeschichte französischer und lothringischer Klöster im 10. und 11. Jahrhundert' *Zs für Social- und Wirthschaftsgeschichte* 1 (1893) 154-90.

715

Platelle, Henri *Le temporel de l'abbaye de Saint-Amand des origines à 1340* (Bibliothèque elzévirienne, NS: Etudes et documents; Paris 1962).

716

Delisle, Léopold 'Enquête sur la fortune des établissements de l'ordre de Saint-Benoît en 1338' *Notices et extraits des manuscrits de la Bibliothèque nationale et autres bibliothèques* 39 (1910) 359-408.

717

Bordeaux, Michèle *Aspects économiques de la vie d'église aux XIVe et XVe siècles* (Bibliothèque d'histoire du droit et droit romain 16; Paris 1969) Deals with monasteries as well as secular churches.

Alsace-Lorraine

718

Perrin, Charles-Edmond *Recherches sur la seigneurie rurale en Lorraine d'après les plus anciens censiers (IXe-XIIe siècle)* (Publications de la faculté des lettres de l'Université de Strasbourg 71; Paris 1935).

719

Dubled, Henri 'Aspects de l'économie cistercienne en Alsace au XIIe siècle' *Rev d'hist ecc* 54 (1959) 765-82.

Cluny

720

Valous, Guy de 'Le domaine de l'abbaye de Cluny aux Xe et XIe siècles' *Annales de l'Académie de Mâcon* 3 S, 22 (1920-1) 299-481 (and separately).

721

Valous, Guy de *Le temporel et la situation financière des établissements de l'ordre de Cluny du XIIe au XIVe siècle, particulièrement dans les provinces françaises* (Archives 41; Ligugé - Paris 1935)
Cf **205**.

722
Schreiber, Georg 'Cluny und die Eigenkirche. Zur Würdigung der Traditionsnotizen des hochmittelalterlichen Frankreich' *Archiv für Urkundenforschung* 17 (1941-2) 359-418, and *Gemeinschaften* 137, 81-138.

723
Sydow, Jürgen 'Cluny und die Anfänge der apostolischen Kammer' *Stud Mitt* 63 (1951) 45-66.

724
Duby, Georges 'Economie domaniale et économie monétaire. Le budget de l'abbaye de Cluny entre 1080 et 1155' *Annales* 7 (1952) 155-71
Cf also his 'Un inventaire des profits de la seigneurie clunisienne à la mort de Pierre le Vénérable' *Petrus Venerabilis* 211, 128-40.

Lyonnais

725
Gaussin, Pierre-Roger 'De la seigneurie rurale à la baronnie. L'abbaye de Savigny en Lyonnais' *Le Moyen Âge* 61 (4 S, 10; 1955) 139-76
Covers tenth to fourteenth centuries.

La Marche

726
Martin, Gabriel 'La Haute-Marche au douzième siècle' *Mémoires de la Société des sciences naturelles et archéologiques de la Creuse* 8 (NS, 3; 1893-4) 47-127
On Cistercian economy and agriculture.

Normandy

727
Sauvage, René Norbert *L'abbaye de Saint-Martin de Troarn au diocèse de Bayeux des origines au seizième siècle* (Mémoires de la Société des antiquaires de Normandie 34 (4 S, 4); Caen - Rouen - Paris 1911)
Pp 125-280 on economic development.

728

Lot, Ferdinand *Etudes critiques sur l'abbaye de Saint-Wandrille* (Bibliothèque de l'Ecole des hautes études 204; Paris 1913)
Economic history of St Wandrille from sixth to sixteenth century.

Germany

729

Fastlinger, Max *Die wirtschaftliche Bedeutung der bayrischen Klöster in
der Zeit der Agilulfinger* (Freiburg B. 1902).

730

Muggenthaler, Hans *Kolonisatorische und wirtschaftliche Tätigkeit eines
deutschen Zisterzienserklosters im XII. und XIII. Jahrhundert* (Deutsche
Geschichtsbücherei 2; Munich 1924)
Waldsassen, founded 1133.

731

Kirchner, Gero 'Probleme der spätmittelalterlichen Klostergrundherrschaft
in Bayern. Landflucht und bäuerliches Erbrecht. Ein Beitrag zur Genesis
des Territorialstaates' *Zs für bayerische Landesgeschichte* 19 (1956) 1-94.

732

Kaller, Gerhard *Wirtschafts- und Besitzgeschichte des Zisterzienserklosters
Otterberg 1144-1561* (Heidelberger Veröffentlichungen 6; Heidelberg
1961).

733

Thiele, Augustinus *Echternach und Himmerod. Beispiele benediktinischer
und zisterziensischer Wirtschaftsführung im 12. und 13. Jahrhundert*
(Forschungen zur Sozial- und Wirtschaftsgeschichte 7; Stuttgart 1964).

Italy

734

Hartmann, Ludo Moritz *Zur Wirtschaftsgeschichte Italiens im frühen
Mittelalter* (Gotha 1904)
Pp 42-73 on economy of Bobbio in ninth century.

735

Gosso, Francesco *Vita economica delle abbazie piemontesi (sec. X-XIV)*
(Analecta gregoriana 22; Rome 1940).

Spain

736
García de Cortázar y Ruiz de Aguirre, José Angel *El dominio del monasterio de San Millán de la Cogolla (siglos X a XIII). Introducción a la historia rural de Castilla altomedieval* (Acta salmanticensia 59; Salamanca 1969).

737
Moreta Velayos, Salustiano *El monasterio de San Pedro de Cardeña. Historia de un dominio monástico castellano (902-1338)* (Acta salmanticensia 63; Salamanca 1971).

Rules and Customs

738
Die grossen Ordensregeln ed Hans Urs von Balthasar (1948) 2nd ed
(Einsiedeln 1961)
Includes chapters on the rules of Basil (Hans Urs von Balthasar), Augustine
(Winfried Hümpfner), Benedict (Franz Faessler), and Francis (Laurentius
Casutt).

EASTERN

739
Besse, Jean-Martial 'Les règles monastiques orientales antérieures au
concile de Chalcédoine' *Revue de l'Orient chrétien* 4 (1899) 465-94.
740
Laun, Ferdinand 'Die beiden Regeln des Basilius, ihre Echtheit und
Entstehung' *Zs für KG* 44 (1925) 1-61.

REGULA BENEDICTI

Cf **10-11, 135, 738, 935**.

741
La règle du Maître ed and trans Adalbert de Vogüé. 2 vols (Sources
chrétiennes 105-106; Paris 1964)
With extensive historical introduction in vol I.

742

La règle de S Benoît ed and trans Adalbert de Vogüé and Jean Neufville
6 vols (Sources chrétiennes 181-186; Paris 1971-2)
The most recent edition, with historical and critical commentary in vols
IV-VI. Cf Eugène Manning in *Rev d'hist ecc* 68 (1973) 457-64.

743

Haeften, Benedictus van *S Benedictus illustratus sive disquisitionum
monasticarum libri XII* (Antwerp 1644)
The longest and still one of the most learned commentaries on the *Regula
Benedicti.*

744

Martène, Edmond *Commentarius in regulam S P Benedicti litteralis,
moralis, historicus* (1690) 2nd ed (Paris 1695)
Also printed with the text of the Rule in *Patrologia latina* 66.

745

Delatte, Paul *Commentaire sur la règle de Saint Benoît* (Paris 1913; Eng
trans by Justin McCann 1921)
On this and other commentaries on the *Regula Benedicti*, both medieval
and modern, see Butler **149**, 177-83; Schmitz **153**, I, 397-405; and Schroll
167, Appendix.

746

Herwegen, Ildefons *Sinn und Geist der Benediktinerregel* (Einsiedeln -
Cologne 1944)
This and **747** are representative modern works on the Rule. Herwegen
interprets it in the light of the charismatic or 'pneumatic' view of
monasticism.

747

Steidle, Basilius *Die Regel St Benedikts* (Beuron 1952)
Interprets the Rule in terms of the religious world of late Antiquity.

REGULA MIXTA

748

O'Carroll, James 'Monastic Rules in Merovingian Gaul' *Studies* 42 (1953)
407-19
On the spread of the *Regula Benedicti* in sixth to eighth centuries.

749

Gougaud, Louis 'Inventaire des règles monastiques irlandaises' *Rev bén*

25 (1908) 167-84, 321-33; 28 (1911) 86-9
Lists 24 rules in all.

750
Clercq, Charles [Carlo] de *La législation religieuse franque de Clovis à Charlemagne. Etude sur les actes de conciles et les capitulaires, les statuts diocésains et les règles monastiques (507-814)* (Université de Louvain: Recueil de travaux publiés par les membres des conférences d'histoire et de philologie, 2 S, 38; Louvain - Paris 1936); and II: *De Louis le Pieux à la fin du IXe siècle (814-900)* (Antwerp 1958)
The text of vol II appeared originally in the *Revue de droit canonique* 4-8 (1954-8).

CUSTOMS

Cf 372.

751
Albers, Bruno *Untersuchungen zu den ältesten Mönchsgewohnheiten. Ein Beitrag zur Benediktinerordensgeschichte des X.-XII. Jahrhunderts* (Veröffentlichungen aus dem kirchenhistorischen Seminar München II, 8; Munich 1905)
The pioneering work, though revised by later research.

752
Corpus consuetudinum monasticarum ed Kassius Hallinger. 7 vols to date (Siegburg 1963ff)
Vol I includes a general introduction, with bibliography, on monastic customaries and this new edition. Cf Jean Leclercq and Réginald Grégoire in *Studi medievali* 3 S, 5 (1964) 658-68; Gregorio Penco in *Bullettino dell' Istituto storico italiano per il medio evo* 77 (1965) 263-73; Cyrille Lambot in *Rev bén* 75 (1965) 151-63; Pascal Ladner in *Zs für schweizerische Kirchengeschichte* 61 (1967) 351-8; Anselm Strittmatter in *Traditio* 25 (1969) 431-57.

CISTERCIANS

753
Bock, Colomban *Les codifications du droit cistercien* (Westmalle [1955])
Collections of articles, separately paginated and with addenda and index, published in *Coll cist* 9-17 (1947-55).

CANONS

Cf 288-9, 291.

754
Amort, Eusebius *Vetus disciplina canonicorum regularium et saecularium* 2 vols paged consecutively (Venice 1747).

755
Egger, Carlo 'De antiquis regulis canonicorum regularium' *Ordo canonicus* 1 (1946) 35-60.

756
Dereine, Charles 'Coutumiers et ordinaires de chanoines réguliers' *Scriptorium* 5 (1951) 107-13; 13 (1959) 244-6.

757
Verheijen, Luc [Melchior] *La règle de Saint Augustin* 2 vols (Paris 1967) Vol I: Manuscript tradition; II: Historical researches.

758
Hocquard, Gaston 'La règle de Saint Chrodegang. Etat de quelques questions' *St Chrodegang* **290**, 55-89.

759
Heijman, Hugo T. 'Untersuchungen ueber die Praemonstratenser-Gewohn-heiten' *Anal praem* 2 (1926) 5-32; 3 (1927) 5-27; 4 (1928) 113-31, 225-41, 351-73, and separately (Tongerloo 1928)
Examines relation of Premonstratensian to Cistercian, Cluniac, and other customs.

The Status of Monks

OBLATION

760
Seidl, Joh. Nep. *Die Gott-Verlobung von Kindern in Mönchs- und Nonnen-Klöstern, oder* de pueris oblatis. *Eine kirchenrechtsgeschichtliche Untersuchung* (Munich 1872)
Not seen.

761
Besse, Jean-Martial 'Du droit d'oblat dans les anciens monastères français' *Rev Mab* 3 (1907) 1-21, 116-33.

762
Deroux, M.-P. *Les origines de l'oblature bénédictine* (Les éditions de la Revue Mabillon 1; Ligugé 1927).

763
Riepenhoff, J. Raphael *Zur Frage des Ursprungs der Verbindlichkeit des Oblateninstituts. Ein Beitrag zur Geschichte des mittelalterlichen Bildungswesens* (Münstersche Beiträge zur Geschichtsforschung, 3 S, 23-24; Münster W. 1939).

764
Lentini, Anselmo 'Note sull'oblazione dei fanciulli nella regola di S Benedetto' *Studia benedictina* **156**, 195-225.

765
Marchal, Jean *Le 'droit d'oblat'. Essai sur une variété de pensionnés monastiques* (Archives 49; Ligugé - Paris 1955).

766
Hofmeister, Philipp 'Die Klaustral-Oblaten' *Stud Mitt* 72 (1961) 5-45.

767

Orlandis, José 'La oblación de niños a los monasterios en la España visigótica' *Yermo* 1 (1963) 33-47 and *Estudios* 487, 53-68; and 'Notas sobre la "oblatio puerorum" en los siglos XI y XII' *Anuario de historia del derecho español* 31 (1961) 163-73 and *Estudios* 487, 205-15.

CONVERSION

Cf 220, 238.

768

Mettler, Adolf 'Laienmönche Laienbrüder Conversen, besonders bei den Hirsauern' *Württembergische Vierteljahrshefte für Landesgeschichte* 41 (1935) 201-53.

769

Hallinger, Kassius 'Woher kommen die Laienbrüder?' *Anal cist* 12 (1956) 1-104

Cf Ernst Werner in *Zs für Geschichtswissenschaft* 6 (1958) 353-61.

770

Hallinger, Kassius 'Ausdrucksformen des Umkehr-Gedankens. Zu den geistigen Grundlagen und den Entwicklungsphasen der Instituta Conversorum' *Stud Mitt* 70 (1959) 169-81.

771

Hofmeister, Philipp 'Die Rechtsverhältnisse der Konversen' *Österreichisches Archiv für Kirchenrecht* 13 (1962) 3-47.

772

Grundmann, Herbert 'Adelsbekehrungen im Hochmittelalter. *Conversi* und *nutriti* im Kloster' *Adel und Kirche. Gerd Tellenbach zum 65. Geburtstag dargebracht von Freunden und Schülern* ed Josef Fleckenstein and Karl Schmid (Freiburg B. - Basel - Vienna 1968) 325-45.

Cistercian Lay-Brothers

773

Hoffmann, Eberhard *Das Konverseninstitut des Cisterzienserordens in seinem Ursprung und seiner Organisation* (Freiburger historische Studien 1; Freiburg S. 1905).

774
[Ducourneau], J. Othon 'De l'institution et des us des convers dans l'ordre de Cîteaux (XIIe et XIIIe siècles)' *Bernard et son temps* **256**, II, 139-201.
775
Donnelly, James S. *The Decline of the Medieval Cistercian Laybrotherhood* (Fordham University Studies, History Series 3; New York 1949).

AD SUCCURRENDUM

776
Gougaud, Louis 'Mourir sous le froc' *Dévotions* **1026**, 129-42.
777
Figueras, Cesáreo M. 'Acerca del rito de la professión monástica medieval "ad succurrendum"' *Liturgica* 2 (1958) 359-400.
778
Valvekens, J. B. 'Fratres et sorores "ad succurrendum"' *Anal praem* 37 (1961) 323-8.
779
Brückner, Wolfgang 'Sterben im Mönchsgewand. Zum Funktionswandel einer Totenkleidsitte' *Kontakte und Grenzen. Probleme der Volks-, Kultur- und Sozialforschung. Festschrift für Gerhard Heilfurth zum 60. Geburtstag* (Göttingen 1969) 259-77.

CONFRATERNITY AND *FAMILIARITAS*

Cf **850-2** on liturgical commemoration.

780
Berlière, Ursmer *Les fraternités monastiques et leur rôle juridique* (Académie royale de Belgique: Classe des lettres et des sciences morales et politiques, Mémoires in -8°, 2 S, 11.3; Brussels 1920).
781
Berlière, Ursmer 'Les confraternités monastiques au moyen âge' *Revue liturgique et monastique* 11 (1926) 134-42; and 'Confréries bénédictines au moyen âge' *ibid* 12 (1927) 135-45.
782
Orlandis, José ' "Traditio corporis et animae". La "familiaritas" en las iglesias y monasterios españoles de la alta edad media' *Anuario de historia del derecho español* 24 (1954) 95-279 and *Estudios* **487**, 219-378.

783

Schmid, Karl and Joachim Wollasch 'Die Gemeinschaft der Lebenden und Verstorbenen in Zeugnissen des Mittelalters. I: Probleme der Erforschung frühmittelalterliche Gedenkbücher. II: Die Überlieferung cluniacensischen Totengedächtnisses' *Frühmittelalterliche Studien* 1 (1967) 365-405 Cf 851.

LEGAL STATUS OF MONKS

784

Landry, Charles *La mort civile des religieux dans l'ancien droit français. Etude historique et critique* (Paris 1900) Studies various monastic incapacities down to eighteenth century.

785

Durtelle de Saint-Sauveur, Edmond *Recherches sur l'histoire de la théorie de la mort civile des religieux des origines au seizième siècle* (Rennes 1910).

786

Kaps, Johannes *Das Testamentrecht der Weltgeistlichen und Ordenspersonen in Rechtsgeschichte, Kirchenrecht und bürgerlichem Recht Deutschlands, Österreichs und der Schweiz* (Munich 1958) Part I (pp 19-115) is historical.

787

Protin, J. 'Profession religieuse et incapacité de posséder selon la doctrine classique' *Ephemerides theologicae lovanienses* 35 (1959) 25-58.

788

Blecker, Michael [Paulin] 'The Civil Rights of the Monk in Roman and Canon Law: The Monk as *Servus*' *American Benedictine Review* 17 (1966) 185-98.

NOVITIATE

789

Hermans, Vincent 'De novitiatu in ordine benedictino-cisterciensi et in iure communi usque ad annum 1335' *Anal cist* 3 (1947) 1-110 Covers both admission to the novitiate and the novitiate.

790

Biedermann, Hermenegild M. 'Novizenunterweisung in Byzanz um die Jahrtausendwende' *Ostkirchliche Studien* 1 (1952) 16-31.

PROFESSION

791
Rothenhäusler, Matthäus 'Zur Aufnahmeordnung der Regula S Benedicti' and Ildefons Herwegen 'Geschichte der benediktinischen Professformel' *Studien zur benediktinischen Profess* (Beiträge 3; Münster W. 1912).

792
Hertling, Ludwig 'Die professio der Kleriker und die Entstehung der drei Gelübde' *Zs für katholische Theologie* 56 (1932) 148-74.

793
Frank, Hieronymus 'Untersuchungen zur Geschichte der benediktinischen Professliturgie im frühen Mittelalter' *Stud Mitt* 63 (1951) 93-139.

794
Hofmeister, Philipp 'Benediktinische Professriten' *Stud Mitt* 74 (1963) 241-85.

795
Leclercq, Jean 'Profession According to the Rule of St Benedict' *Rule and Life: An Interdisciplinary Symposium* ed M. Basil Pennington (Cistercian Studies Series 12; Spencer, Mass. 1971) 117-49.

CONSECRATION

796
Molitor, Raphael 'Von der Mönchsweihe in der lateinischen Kirche' *Theologie und Glaube* 16 (1924) 584-612.

797
Casel, Odo 'Die Mönchsweihe' *Jahrbuch für Liturgiewissenschaft* 5 (1925) 1-47
Covers both East and West.

798
Oppenheim, Philipp 'Mönchsweihe und Taufritus' *Miscellanea liturgica in honorem L. Cuniberti Mohlberg* (Bibliotheca 'Ephemerides liturgicae' 22-23; Rome 1948-9) I, 259-82.

TONSURE

799
Chamillard, Gaston *De corona, tonsura et habitu clericorum* (Paris 1659)
Not seen.

800

Gobillot, Philippe 'Sur la tonsure chrétienne et ses prétendues origines païennes' *Rev d'hist ecc* 21 (1925) 399-454
Mostly on fourth to sixth centuries, but with some later material.

801

Bock, Colomban 'Tonsure monastique et tonsure cléricale' *Revue de droit canonique* 2 (1952) 373-406.

CLOTHING

Cf 813-14.

802

Oppenheim, Philipp *Das Mönchskleid im christlichen Altertum* (Römische Quartalschrift für christliche Altertumskunde und für Kirchengeschichte, Supplementheft 28; Freiburg B. 1931); and *Symbolik und religiöse Wertung des Mönchskleides im christlichen Altertum, vornehmlich nach zeugnissen christlicher Schriftsteller der Ostkirche* (Theologie des christlichen Ostens: Texte und Untersuchungen 2; Münster W. 1932)
On these two works cf Louis Th. Lefort in *Rev d'hist ecc* 28 (1932) 851-3 and especially Placide de Meester in *Ephemerides liturgicae* 47 (1933) 446-58.

CHASTITY AND CELIBACY

Cf 322-6, 821, 942.

803

Kötting, Bernhard *Der Zölibat in der alten Kirche* (Schriften der Gesellschaft zur Förderung der westfälischen Wilhelms-Universität zu Münster 61; Münster W. 1968).

804

Chastity. Being the English Version of 'La chasteté' in 'Problèmes de la religieuse d'aujourd'hui ' trans Lancelot C. Sheppard (London 1955)
French version not seen. See especially articles on chastity in the Greek Fathers (Olivier Rousseau) and in the Latin West (Michel Olphe-Galliard).

OBEDIENCE

805
Rousseau, Olivier 'Obéissance et hiérarchie d'après l'ancienne tradition monastique' *La vie spirituelle: Supplément* 6 (1953) 283-98.

806
Bock, Colomban *La promesse d'obéissance ou la 'professio regularis'* (Westmalle 1955).

807
Capelle, Catherine *Le voeu d'obéissance des origines au XIIe siècle. Etude juridique* (Bibliothèque d'histoire du droit et droit romain 2; Paris 1959).

STABILITY

808
Rothenhäusler, Matthäus 'Ältestes Mönchtum und klösterliche Beständigkeit' *Benediktinische Monatschrift* 3 (1921) 87-95, 223-37; 'Die Beständigkeit des Benediktiners' *ibid* 345-57; and 'Die rechtlichen Wirkungen der benediktinischen Beständigkeit' *ibid* 440-54
The first article goes down to the seventh century.

809
Herman, Emil 'La "stabilitas loci" nel monachismo bizantino' *Orientalia christiana periodica* 21 (1955) 116-42.

TRANSITUS

810
Hofmeister, Philipp 'Der Übertritt in eine andere religiöse Genossenschaft' *Archiv für katholisches Kirchenrecht* 108 (1928) 419-81.

811
Fina, Kurt ' "Ovem suam requirere". Eine Studie zur Geschichte des Ordenswechsels im 12. Jahrhundert' *Augustiniana* 7 (1957) 33-56.

Life and Activities

GENERAL

812
Thomassin, Louis *Ancienne et nouvelle discipline de l'église* (1725) ed
M. André. 7 vols (Bar-le-Duc 1864-7)
Deals with many questions of monastic discipline and organization, both
inside and outside the monastery.
813
Gougaud, Louis *Anciennes coutumes claustrales* (Moines et monastères 8;
Ligugé 1930)
See **568** and chapters on sign language, clothing, phlebotomy, death,
behaviour in choir, etc, with a bibliography of rules and customs used.
814
Dimier, Marie-Anselme 'Observances monastiques' *Anal cist* 11 (1955)
149-98
Sections on holy office, silence, abstinence, work, habit, manners within
the monastery, 'Mandatum', making hosts, travelling, and monastic bishops.
815
Dubois, Jacques 'La vie des moines dans les prieurés du moyen âge'
Lettre de Ligugé 1969.1 (no 133) 10-33.

SILENCE

Cf **814**.

816
Salmon, Pierre 'Le silence religieux. Pratique et théorie' *Mélanges bén*
157, 13-57.

SIGN LANGUAGE

Cf 813.

817
Van Rijnberk, Gerard *Le langage par signes chez les moines* (Amsterdam 1953).

DIET

Cf 814, 1026-7.

818
Bishop, Edmund 'The Method and Degree of Fasting and Abstinence of the Black Monks in England before the Reformation' *Downside Review* 43 (1925) 184-237
Written in 1884 and published posthumously.

819
Volk, Paul 'Das Abstinenzindult von 1523 für die Benediktinerklöster der Mainz-Bamberger Provinz' *Rev bén* 40 (1928) 333-63.

820
Semmler, Josef ' "Volatilia". Zu den benediktinischen Consuetudines des 9. Jahrhunderts ' *Stud Mitt* 69 (1958) 163-76.

821
Rousselle, Aline 'Abstinence et continence dans les monastères de Gaule méridionale à la fin de l'antiquité et au début du moyen âge. Etude d'un régime alimentaire et de sa fonction' *Hommage à André Dupont (1897-1972)* (Montpellier 1974) 239-54.

CURA CORPORIS

822
Casoli, Vincenzo 'Fra i monachi. Rievocazioni d'igiene e di medicina cenobitica' *Rivista di storia delle scienze mediche e naturali* 14 (Anno 23; 1932) 241-57
Hygiene, work, sleep, etc.

823
Zimmermann, Gerd *Ordensleben und Lebensstandard. Die Cura corporis*

in den Ordensvorschriften des abendländischen Hochmittelalters (Beiträge 32; Münster W. 1973).

LITURGY

Cf **324-6, 488, 793, 814, 912.**

824
Martène, Edmond *De antiquis monachorum ritibus libri quinque* (1690) 2nd ed in vol IV of *De antiquis ecclesiae ritibus* 4 vols (Antwerp 1736-8) With extensive citations from sources, some of which are now lost.

825
Bishop, Edmund *Liturgica historica. Papers on the Liturgy and Religious Life of the Western Church* (Oxford 1918) 28 articles, including many of monastic interest.

826
Hilpisch, Stephanus 'Chorgebet und Frömmigkeit im Spätmittelalter' *Heilige Überlieferung. Ausschnitte aus der Geschichte des Mönchtums und des heiligen Kultes dem hochwürdigsten Herrn Abte von Maria Laach ... Ildefons Herwegen ... dargeboten von Freunden, Verehren, Schülern* ed Odo Casel (Beiträge: Supplementband; Münster W. 1938) 263-84.

827
Shepherd, Massey H., Jr 'The Development of Monastic Worship' *The Anglican Theological Review* 21 (1939) 1-21.

828
Penco, Gregorio 'Per la storia liturgica del monachesimo italico nei secoli VII-IX. Correnti ed influssi' *Rivista liturgica* 44 (1957) 168-81.

829
Leclercq, Jean 'Culte liturgique et prière intime dans le monachisme au moyen âge' *La Maison-Dieu* 69 (1962) 39-55 and *Sources* **946.**

Liturgies of the Orders

Cf **292, 955.**

830
King, Archdale A. *Liturgies of the Religious Orders* (London - New York - Toronto 1955) Carthusian, Cistercian, Premonstratensian, and Gilbertine rites.

831
Canivez, Joseph-Marie 'Le rite cistercien' *Ephemerides liturgicae* 63 (1949) 276-311.

832
Marosszéki, Solutor 'Les origines du chant cistercien' *Anal cist* 8 (1952) vii-xvi, 1-179.

833
Waddell, Chrysogonus 'The Early Cistercian Experience of Liturgy' *Rule and Life: An Interdisciplinary Symposium* ed M. Basil Pennington (Cistercian Studies Series 12; Spencer, Mass. 1971) 77-115.

834
Lefèvre, Placide F. *La liturgie de Prémontré. Histoire, formulaire, chant et cérémoniale* (Bibliotheca analectorum praemonstratensium 1; Louvain 1957).

Early Monks

835
Dekkers, Eligius 'Les anciens moines cultivaient-ils la liturgie?' *Vom christlichen Mysterium. Gesammelte Arbeiten zum Gedächtnis von Odo Casel OSB* ed Anton Mayer, Johannes Quasten, and Burkhard Neunheuser (Düsseldorf 1951) 97-114
This influential article has been republished and translated several times: cf Veilleux **836**, xxiv. An English translation is in *Coll cist* 22 (1960) 120-37, together with his article 'Moines et liturgie' *ibid* 329-40.

836
Veilleux, Armand *La liturgie dans le cénobitisme pachômien au quatrième siècle* (Stud Ans 57; Rome 1968).

837
Marx, Michael *Incessant Prayer in Ancient Monastic Literature* (Facultas theologica S Anselmi de Urbe; Rome 1946).

Office

838
Hausherr, Irénée 'Opus Dei' *Miscellanea Guillaume de Jerphanion* (Orientalia christiana periodica 13; Rome 1947) I, 195-218
On the background and meaning of this term in early monastic usage.

839
Heiming, Odilo 'Zum monastischen Offizium von Kassianus bis Kolumbanus' *Archiv für Liturgiewissenschaft* 7 (1961) 89-156
Deals with early rules and practice in both East and West.

840
Vogüé, Adalbert de 'Le sens de l'office divin d'après la règle de S Benoît' *Revue d'ascétique et de mystique* 42 (1966) 389-404; 43 (1967) 21-33.

841
Lejay, Paul 'Les accroissements de l'office quotidien' *Revue du clergé français* 40 (1904) 113-41.

842
Luykx, Boniface 'L'influence des moines sur l'office paroissial' *La Maison-Dieu* 51 (1957) 55-81.

843
Rouillard, Philippe 'Temps et rhythmes de la prière dans le monachisme ancien' *La Maison-Dieu* 64 (1960) 32-52.

Breviary

844
Bäumer, Suitbert *Histoire du bréviaire* (1895) ed and trans Réginald Biron. 2 vols (Paris 1905).

845
The Monastic Breviary of Hyde Abbey, Winchester ed John B. L. Tolhurst 6 vols (Henry Bradshaw Society 69-71, 76, 78, 80; London 1932-42)
Vol VI consists of an *Introduction to the English Monastic Breviaries.*

846
Salmon, Pierre *L'office divin. Histoire de la formation du bréviaire* (Lex orandi 27; Paris 1959).

Liturgical Hours

847
Froger, Jacques *Les origines de Prime* (Bibliotheca 'Ephemerides liturgicae' 19; Rome 1946)
Gives special attention to the work of Cassian.

848
Gindele, Corbinian 'Die Struktur der Nokturnen in den lateinischen

Mönchsregeln vor und um St Benedikt' *Rev bén* 64 (1954) 9-27.

849

Baumstark, Anton *Nocturna Laus. Typen frühchristlicher Vigilienfeier und ihr Fortleben vor allem im römischen und monastischen Ritus* (Liturgie-wissenschaftliche Quellen und Forschungen 32; Münster W. 1957)
Based on the work of Odilo Heiming.

Liturgical Commemoration

Cf **780-3** on confraternity and *familiaritas*.

850

Ebner, Adalbert *Die klösterlichen Gebets-Verbrüderungen bis zum Aus-gange des karolingischen Zeitalters* (Regensburg - New York - Cincinnati 1890).

851

Jorden, Willibald *Das cluniazensische Totengedächtniswesen vornehmlich unter den drei ersten Äbten Berno, Odo und Aymard (910-954)* (Münster-ische Beiträge zur Theologie 15; Münster W. 1930)
Cf Johannes Ramackers in *Quellen und Forschungen aus italienischen Archiven und Bibliotheken* 23 (1931-2) 22-52.

852

Huyghebaert, Nicolas *Les documents nécrologiques* (Typologie des sources du moyen âge occidental 4 [A-VI-A.1*]; Turnhout 1972).

MONASTIC PRIESTHOOD

853

Winandy, Jacques 'Les moines et le sacerdoce' *La vie spirituelle* 80 (1949) 23-36.

854

Dalmais, Irénée-Henri 'Sacerdoce et monachisme dans l'Orient chrétien' *La vie spirituelle* 80 (1949) 37-49.

855

Lafontaine, Paul-Henri *L'évêque d'ordination des religieux des débuts du monachisme à la mort de Louis le Pieux (840)* (Universitas catholica ottaviensis: Dissertationes, Series canonica 22; Ottawa 1951).

856
Rousseau, Olivier 'Sacerdoce et monachisme' *Etudes sur le sacrement de l'ordre* (Lex orandi 22; Paris 1957) 216-31.

857
Leclercq, Jean 'Le sacerdoce des moines' *Irénikon* 36 (1963) 5-40 and *Chances* 946
Several reprints and translations.

858
Nussbaum, Otto *Kloster, Priestermönch und Privatmesse. Ihr Verhältnis im Westen von den Anfängen bis zum hohen Mittelalter* (Theophaneia 14; Bonn 1961)
Cf the criticism by Angelus Häussling in *Zs für katholische Theologie* 85 (1963) 75-83.

859
Priestertum und Mönchtum ed Theodor Bogler (Liturgie und Mönchtum 29; Maria Laach 1961)
7 articles primarily of modern concern, including Theodor Bogler 'Mönchschor und Presbyterium,' pp 56-63.

860
Grégoire, Réginald 'La communion des moines-prêtres à la messe d'après les coutumiers monastiques médiévaux' *Sacris erudiri* 18 (1967-8) 524-49.

MONK-BISHOPS

Cf 814.

861
Frank, Hieronymus *Die Klosterbischöfe des Frankenreiches* (Beiträge 17; Münster W. 1932).

862
Oliger, Paul Remy *Les évêques réguliers* (Museum lessianum: Section historique 18; Paris - Louvain 1958).

863
Rousseau, Philip 'The Spiritual Authority of the "Monk-Bishop": Eastern Elements in some Western Hagiography of the Fourth and Fifth Centuries' *Journal of Theological Studies* NS, 22 (1971) 380-419.

PASTORAL WORK

864

Beck, Egerton 'Regulars and the Parochial System in Mediaeval England' *Dublin Review* 172 (1923) 235-51
Covers twelfth to fourteenth centuries.

865

Berlière, Ursmer 'L'exercice du ministère paroissial par les moines dans le haut moyen-âge' *Rev bén* 39 (1927) 227-50; and 'L'exercice du ministère paroissial par les moines du XIIe au XVIIIe siècle' *ibid* 340-64.

866

Schreiber, Georg 'Gregor VII., Cluny, Cîteaux, Prémontré zu Eigenkirche, Parochie, Seelsorge' *Sav-Zs, Kan Abt* 34 (1947) 31-171 and *Gemeinschaften* 137, 283-370.

867

Hofmeister, Philipp 'Mönchtum und Seelsorge bis zum 13. Jahrhundert' *Stud Mitt* 65 (1953-4) 209-73.

868

Schmale, Franz-Josef 'Kanonie, Seelsorge, Eigenkirche' *Historisches Jahrbuch* 78 (1959) 38-63.

869

Chibnall, Marjorie 'Monks and Pastoral Work: A Problem in Anglo-Norman History' *Journal of Ecclesiastical History* 18 (1967) 165-72.

CHARITABLE WORK

870

Falk, F. 'Die Sorge für die *Peregrini et pauperes* in den alten Klöstern' *Historisch-politische Blätter für das katholische Deutschland* 114 (1894) 340-50.

871

Schönfeld, Walther 'Die Xenodochien in Italien und Frankreich im frühen Mittelalter' *Sav-Zs, Kan Abt* 12 (1922) 1-54.

872

Lallemand, Léon *Histoire de la charité* 4 vols [IV in 2 parts] (Paris 1902-12)
Vol II: *Les neuf premiers siècles de l'ère chrétienne*; III: *Le moyen âge (du Xe au XVIe siècle)*.

873

Lesne, Emile *Les églises et les monastères centres d'accueil, d'exploitation et de peuplement* (Lille 1943)

The final, posthumous volume of **662**.

874

Atti del primo congresso europeo di storia ospitaliera, 6-12 giugno 1960 (Reggio Emilia 1962)

Includes articles on canons (Cosimo Damiano Fonseca) and several on monks and hospitality.

875

Mollat, Michel 'Les moines et les pauvres, XIe-XIIe siècles' *Monachesimo* **221**, 193-215.

LITERATURE AND LEARNING

876

Mabillon, Jean *Traité des études monastiques* (Paris 1691)

The classic treatise on monastic learning, written in reply to the criticisms of Armand de Rancé.

877

Leclercq, Jean *L'amour des lettres et le désir de Dieu. Initiation aux auteurs monastiques du moyen âge* (1957) 2nd ed (Paris 1963; Eng trans by Catherine Misrahi 1961).

878

Gorce, Denys *La lectio divina des origines du cénobitisme à Saint Benoît et Cassiodore*, I: *Saint Jérôme et la lecture sacrée dans le milieu ascétique romain* (Wépion-sur-Meuse - Paris 1925)

No more published.

879

Mohrmann, Christine 'Le rôle des moines dans la transmission du patrimoine latin' *Mémorial* **416**, 185-98.

880

Leclercq, Jean 'Y a-t-il une culture monastique?' *Monachesimo* **161**, 339-56 and *Témoins* **946**.

881

Los monjes y los estudios (IV Semana de estudios monasticos, Poblet 1961; Poblet 1963)

22 articles on monastic attitudes to learning from the beginnings down to the seventeenth century.

882
Koperska, Apollonia *Die Stellung der religiösen Orden zu den Profan-wissenschaften im 12. und 13. Jahrhundert* (Freiburg S. 1914).

883
Legge, Mary Dominica *Anglo-Norman in the Cloisters. The Influence of the Orders upon Anglo-Norman Literature* (Edinburgh University Publications: Language and Literature 2; Edinburgh 1950).

884
Lawrence, Clifford H. 'Stephen of Lexington and Cistercian University Studies in the Thirteenth Century' *Journal of Ecclesiastical History* 11 (1960) 164-78.

885
Kristeller, Paul Oskar 'The Contribution of Religious Orders to Renaissance Thought and Learning' *American Benedictine Review* 21 (1970) 1-55, revised repr in *Medieval Aspects of Renaissance Learning* ed Edward P. Mahoney (Duke Monographs in Medieval and Renaissance Studies 1; Durham, N.C. 1974) 95-158
With appendix of humanist members of religious orders.

SCHOOLS

886
Maître, Léon *Les écoles épiscopales et monastiques de l'Occident depuis Charlemagne jusqu'à Philippe-Auguste (768-1180). Etude historique sur la filiation des écoles, la condition des maîtres et des élèves, et le programme des études avant la création des universités* (Paris 1866; repr in Archives 26 [1924]).

887
Aspinwall, William B. *Les écoles épiscopales [et] monastiques de l'ancienne province ecclésiastique de Sens du VIᵉ au XIIᵉ siècle. Les maîtres et les matières de l'enseignement* (Paris 1904).

888
Berlière, Ursmer 'Ecoles claustrales au moyen âge' *Académie royale de Belgique: Bulletin de la classe des lettres* 5 S, 7 (1921) 550-72.

889
Lesne, Emile *Les écoles de la fin du VIIIᵉ siècle à la fin du XIIᵉ* (Lille 1940)
Vol V of **662**.

890

Delhaye, Philippe 'L'organisation scolaire au XIIe siècle' *Traditio* 5
(1947) 211-68
Pp 225-38 on monastic schools.

891

Bardy, Gustave 'Les origines des écoles monastiques en Orient' *Mélanges
Joseph de Ghellinck*, I: *Antiquité* (Museum lessianum: Section historique
13; Gembloux 1951) 293-309; and 'Les origines des écoles monastiques
en Occident' *Sacris erudiri* 5 (1953) 86-104.

892

Riché, Pierre *Education et culture dans l'Occident barbare, VIe-VIIIe siècles*
(1962) 3rd ed (Patristica Sorbonensia 4; Paris 1973).

LIBRARIES

893

Leistle, David 'Ueber Klosterbibliotheken des Mittelalters' *Stud Mitt* 36
(1915) 197-228, 357-77.

894

Lesne, Emile *Les livres, 'scriptoria' et bibliothèques du commencement
du VIIIe à la fin du XIe siècle* (Lille 1938)
Vol IV of 662.

895

Christ, Karl 'Mittelalterliche Biblioteksordnungen für Frauenklöster'
Zentralblatt für Bibliothekswesen 59 (1942) 1-29.

896

Kottje, Raymund 'Klosterbibliotheken und monastische Kultur in der
zweiten Hälfte des 11. Jahrhunderts' *Zs für KG* 80 (1969) 145-62 and
Monachesimo 221, 351-70.

897

The English Library before 1700 ed Francis Wormald and C. E. Wright
(London 1958)
Includes chapter by Francis Wormald on 'The Monastic Library'.

898

Nortier [-Marchand], Geneviève *Les bibliothèques médiévales des abbayes
bénédictines de Normandie* (Caen 1966 and Paris 1967)
Reprints of articles in the *Rev Mab* on the libraries of Fécamp, Le Bec,
Mont St-Michel, etc.

899

Löffler, Klemens *Deutsche Klosterbibliotheken* (1918) 2nd ed (Bücherei der Kultur und Geschichte 27; Bonn - Leipzig 1922).

MEDICINE

900

Schipperges, Heinrich *Die Benediktiner in der Medizin des frühen Mittelalters* (Erfurter theologische Schriften 7; Leipzig 1964).

ART AND ARCHITECTURE

901

Swartwout, Robert E. *The Monastic Craftsman: An Inquiry into the Services of Monks to Art in Britain and in Europe North of the Alps during the Middle Ages* (Cambridge 1932).

902

Weisbach, Werner *Religiöse Reform und mittelalterliche Kunst* (Einsiedeln - Zurich 1945).

903

Zarnecki, George *The Monastic Achievement* (London - New York 1972) First separate edition of an essay published in 1966 and described by the author as 'not a history of monasticism or a history of monastic art, but ... a little of both.'

Monastic Plans

904

Schlosser, Julius [von] *Die abendländische Klosteranlage des früheren Mittelalters* (Vienna 1889).

905

Hager, Georg 'Zur Geschichte der abendländischen Klosteranlage' *Zs für christliche Kunst* 14 (1901) 97-106, 139-46, 167-86, 193-204.

906

Studien zum St Galler Klosterplan ed Johannes Duft (Mitteilungen zur vaterländischen Geschichte 42; St Gallen 1962) 11 articles on various aspects of the St Gall plan.

907

Dimier, Marie-Anselme *Recueil de plans d'églises cisterciennes* 2 vols
(Commission d'histoire de l'ordre de Cîteaux 1; Grignan - Paris 1949); and
Supplément 2 vols (Paris - Aiguebelle 1967).

Aerial Photography

908

Knowles, David and John K. S. St Joseph *Monastic Sites from the Air*
(Cambridge Air Surveys 1; Cambridge 1952).

909

Norman, Edward R. and John K. S. St Joseph *The Early Development of
Irish Society: The Evidence of Aerial Photography* (Cambridge Air
Surveys 3; Cambridge 1969)
Chapter 5 on early Christian sites, mostly monastic.

Architecture

910

Lenoir, Albert *Architecture monastique* 2 vols (Collection de documents
inédits sur l'histoire de France [5]; Paris 1852-6).

911

Conant, Kenneth J. *Benedictine Contributions to Church Architecture*
(Wimmer Lecture 1; Latrobe, Pa. 1949)
Cf also his more general work *Carolingian and Romanesque Architecture:
800 to 1200* (1959) 3rd ed (Pelican History of Art Z 13; Harmondsworth
1974).

912

Heitz, Carol *Recherches sur les rapports entre architecture et liturgie à
l'époque carolingienne* (Bibliothèque générale de l'Ecole pratique des
hautes études, VIe section; Paris 1963)
Studies especially the 'église-porche' (*Westwerk*) at St Riquier.

913

Braunfels, Wolfgang *Monasteries of Western Europe: The Architecture of
the Orders* (1969) revised Eng trans by Alastair Laing (London -
Princeton 1972)
Comes down to modern times.

France

914
Stoddard, Whitney S. *Monastery and Cathedral in France: Medieval Architecture, Sculpture, Stained Glass, Manuscripts, the Art of the Church Treasures* (Middletown, Conn. 1966).

British Isles

915
Cranage, David H. S. *The Home of the Monk: An Account of English Monastic Life and Buildings in the Middle Ages* (1926) 3rd ed (Cambridge 1934).

916
Palmer, Roger Liddesdale *English Monasteries in the Middle Ages. An Outline of Monastic Architecture and Custom from the Conquest to the Suppression* (London 1930).

917
Crossley, Frederick H. *The English Abbey: Its Life and Work in the Middle Ages* (1935) 3rd ed with new foreword (London 1949)
Architectural in emphasis, but with chapters on monastic life and organization.

918
Dickinson, John C. 'Les constructions des premiers chanoines réguliers en Angleterre' *Cahiers de civilisation médiévale* 10 (1967) 179-98.

919
Leask, Harold G. *Irish Churches and Monastic Buildings* 3 vols (Dundalk 1955-60)
Vol I: First Phases and Romanesque; II: Gothic to 1400; III: Late Gothic.

St Gall

Cf **906**.

920
Clark, James M. *The Abbey of St Gall as a Centre of Literature and Art* (Cambridge 1926).

Reichenau

921

Die Kultur der Abtei Reichenau ed Konrad Beyerle. 2 vols (Munich 1925) Collected articles, including a history of Reichenau from its foundation to 1427 by Beyerle (pp 55-212).

922

Dodwell, Charles R. and Derek H. Turner *Reichenau Reconsidered: A Reassessment of the Place of Reichenau in Ottonian Art* (Warburg Institute Surveys 2; London 1965) Argues role of Reichenau has been exaggerated.

Cluny and the Cluniacs

923

Mercier, Fernand *Les primitifs français. La peinture clunysienne en Bourgogne à l'époque romane* (Paris 1931).

924

Evans, Joan *The Romanesque Architecture of the Order of Cluny* (Cambridge 1938).

925

Evans, Joan *Cluniac Art of the Romanesque Period* (Cambridge 1950).

926

Schapiro, Meyer *The Parma Ildefonsus: A Romanesque Illuminated Manuscript from Cluny and Related Works* (Monographs on Archaeology and Fine Arts sponsored by the Archaeological Institute of America and the College Art Association of America 11; [New York] 1964).

927

Conant, Kenneth J. *Cluny. Les églises et la maison du chef d'ordre* (Mediaeval Academy of America, Publication 77; Cambridge, Mass. - Mâcon 1968) Cf François Salet in *Bulletin monumental* 126 (1968) 235-92 and Alain Erlande-Brandenburg *ibid* 293-322; also Conant in *Speculum* 45 (1970) 1-39; *Cahiers de civilisation médiévale* 14 (1971) 341-7; *Rev bén* 81 (1971) 60-6; *Monumentum* 7 (1971) 11-33.

Cistercians

928
Aubert, Marcel and Geneviève Aliette [de Rohan-Chabot, marquise] de
Maillé *L'architecture cistercienne en France* (1943) 2nd ed 2 vols (Paris
1947).

929
Hahn, Hanno *Die frühe Kirchenbaukunst der Zisterzienser. Untersuchungen
zur Baugeschichte von Kloster Eberbach im Rheingau und ihren europäischen
Analogien im 12. Jahrhundert* (Frankfurter Forschungen zur Architektur-
geschichte 1; Berlin 1957)
Cf Angiola Maria Romanini in *Povertà* 1002, 191-225 and (on this and
other recent works on Cistercian architecture) Kolumban Spahr in *Cistercienser-Chronik* 65 (1958) 41-59 and Leopold Grill in *Anal cist* 16 (1960)
293-307.

930
Eydoux, Henri-Paul *L'architecture des églises cisterciennes d'Allemagne*
(Travaux et mémoires des Instituts français en Allemagne 1; Paris 1952).

931
Fraccaro de Longhi, Lelia *L'architettura delle chiese cisterciensi italiane*
(Pubblicazioni della facoltà di filosofia e lettere dell'Università di Pavia;
Milan 1958).

932
Oursel, Charles *La miniature du XIIe siècle à l'abbaye de Cîteaux d'après
les manuscrits de la bibliothèque de Dijon* (Dijon 1926)
Cf also his *Miniatures cisterciennes (1109-1134)* (Mâcon 1960), which
covers much of the same material.

Other Orders

933
Crozet, René 'L'architecture de l'ordre de Grandmont en Poitou, Saintonge
et Angoumois' *Bulletins et mémoires de la Société archéologique et
historique de la Charente* 1944 (II) 221-41.

934
Gaborit, Jean-René 'Les plus anciens monastères de l'ordre de Vallombreuse
(1037-1115). Etude archéologique' *Ecole français de Rome: Mélanges
d'archéologie et d'histoire* 76 (1964) 451-90; 77 (1965) 179-208.

Monastic Ideals and Spirituality

BIBLIOGRAPHY

Cf 22, 947.

935
Problemi e orientamenti di spiritualità monastica, biblica e liturgica ed
Cipriano Vagaggini et al (Rome 1961)
Cf *Rev bén* 72 (1962) 385-7. Includes bibliographical studies on the
Benedictine Rule (Gregorio Penco), twelfth-century Benedictine spiritu-
ality (Mariano Magrassi), and twelfth-century Cistercian spirituality
(Enrico Baccetti).

936
Penco, Gregorio 'Rassegna di studi sulla spiritualità monastica medievale'
Rivista di storia e letteratura religiosa 2 (1966) 93-115
Discusses works published in 1950s and early 1960s.

GENERAL

Cf 41, 292, 826.

937
Pourrat, Pierre *La spiritualité chrétienne*, II: *Le moyen âge* (Paris 1921;
Eng trans by S. P. Jacques 1924)
Cf Marcel Viller in *Revue d'ascétique et de mystique* 3 (1922) 72-81.

938
Vernet, Félix *La spiritualité médiévale* (Bibliothèque catholique des
sciences religieuses 33; Paris 1929; Eng trans 1930).

939

Wilmart, André *Auteurs spirituels et textes dévots du moyen âge latin.*
Etudes d'histoire littéraire (Paris 1932)
25 of Wilmart's most important articles; cf the bibliography of his works
by Jeanne Bignami Odier, Louis Brou, and André Vernet (Rome 1953).

940

Kirk, Kenneth E. *The Vision of God: The Christian Doctrine of the
'Summum Bonum'* (1931) 2nd ed (Bampton Lectures 1928; London
1932).

941

Schreiber, Georg 'Monasterium und Frömmigkeit' *Zs für Aszese und
Mystik (Geist und Leben)* 16 (1941) 19-32
Not seen.

942

Rousseau, Olivier *Monachisme et vie religieuse d'après l'ancienne tradition
de l'église* (Irénikon, NS, 7; Chevetogne [1957])
Ideals of perfection, virginity, common life, poverty, obedience, etc,
through twelfth century.

943

Genicot, Léopold *La spiritualité médiévale* (Je sais - je crois 40.4; Paris
1958).

944

Théologie de la vie monastique. Etudes sur la tradition patristique
(Théologie. Etudes publiées sous la direction de la faculté de théologie S. J.
de Lyon-Fourvière 49; Paris 1961)
Cf François Vandenbroucke in *Stud mon* 4 (1962) 369-89. Includes articles
on Origen (Henri Crouzel), Pachomius (Heinrich Bacht), Apophthegmata
patrum (Jean-Claude Guy), Ephraim the Syrian (Louis Leloir), Basil (Jean
Gribomont), Gregory of Nazianzus (Jean Plagnieux), Gregory of Nyssa
(Jean Daniélou), Chrysostom (Jean-Marie Leroux), Jerome (Paul Antin),
Augustine (Melchior Verheijen), Cassian (Adalbert de Vogüé), Theodoret
and Syrian monasticism (Pierre Canivet), Pseudo-Denis (René Roques),
Gregory the Great (Robert Gillet), Isidore of Seville (Jacques Fontaine),
Visigothic authors (Manuel C. Díaz y Díaz), John Climacus (Irénée Haus-
herr), Theodore of Studium (Julien Leroy), early Middle Ages and Cluny
(Jean Leclercq), Damiani (Giovanni Miccoli), Guigo of La Chartreuse,
Bernard (Placide Deseille), Aelred of Rievaulx (Charles Dumont). A com-
panion volume on modern and contemporary monastic writers was published in Archives 50 (1961).

945

Leclercq, Jean, François Vandenbroucke, and Louis Bouyer *La spiritualité du moyen âge* (Histoire de la spiritualité chrétienne 2; Paris 1961; Eng trans 1968).

946

Leclercq, Jean *Aux sources de la spiritualité occidentale. Etapes et constantes* (Tradition et spiritualité 4; Paris 1964); *Témoins de la spiritualité occidentale* (Tradition et spiritualité 5; Paris 1965); and *Chances de la spiritualité occidentale* (Lumière de la foi 23; Paris 1966)
Collected articles, some of them revised; see **208, 226, 560, 829, 857, 880, 1011**.

947

Peifer, Claude J. *Monastic Spirituality* (New York 1966)
Classified bibliography on pp 479-524.

948

Historia de la espiritualidad, A: *Espiritualidad católica*, I: *Espiritualidades bíblica, de los primeros siglos cristianos y de la edad media* (Barcelona 1969)
Includes sections on early monastic spirituality (García M. Colombás), medieval literary spirituality (Lope Cilleruelo), and medieval monastic spirituality (José Mattoso); cf Tomás Moral in *Rev d'hist ecc* 67 (1972) 423-36.

949

Ladner, Gerhart B. *The Idea of Reform: Its Impact on Christian Thought and Action in the Age of the Fathers* (Cambridge, Mass. 1959)
Part III: 'Monasticism as a Vehicle of the Christian Idea of Reform in the Age of the Fathers'.

MONASTIC SPIRITUALITY IN VERNACULAR POETRY

950

Buttell, Marie Pierre *Religious Ideology and Christian Humanism in German Cluniac Verse* (Catholic University of America, Studies in German 21; Washington 1948).

951

Rupp, Heinz *Deutsche religiöse Dichtungen des 11. und 12. Jahrhunderts* (Freiburg 1958)
Denies Cluniac nature of German religious poetry.

952
Meissburger, Gerhard *Grundlagen zum Verständnis der deutschen Mönchs-dichtung im 11. und 12. Jahrhundert* (Munich 1970).

MYSTICISM

953
Butler, Edward Cuthbert *Western Mysticism: The Teaching of SS Augustine, Gregory and Bernard on Contemplation and the Contemplative Life* (1922) 2nd ed with 'Afterthoughts' (London 1927; repr with intro by David Knowles 1967).

954
Besse, Jean-Martial *Les mystiques bénédictins des origines au XIIIe siècle* (Collection pax 6; Paris - Maredsous 1922).

CLUNY

955
Spiritualità cluniacense, 12-15 ottobre 1958 (Convegni del Centro di studi sulla spiritualità medievale 2; Todi 1960)
See **207**. Includes among others article on Cluniac liturgy by Philibert Schmitz.

CISTERCIANS

956
Bouyer, Louis *La spiritualité de Cîteaux* (Paris 1954; Eng trans by Elizabeth A. Livingstone under the title *The Cistercian Heritage* 1958).

CANONS

957
Dereine, Charles 'La spiritualité "apostolique" des premiers fondateurs d'Affligem (1083-1100)' *Rev d'hist ecc* 54 (1959) 41-65.

958
Schreiber, Georg 'Praemonstratenserkultur des 12. Jahrhunderts' *Anal praem* 16 (1940) 41-107; 17 (1941) 5-33.

959

Petit, François *La spiritualité des Prémontrés aux XIIe et XIIIe siècles* (Etudes de théologie et d'histoire de la spiritualité 10; Paris 1947).

BYZANTINE

960

Holl, Karl *Enthusiasmus und Bussgewalt beim griechischen Mönchtum. Eine Studie zu Symeon dem Neuen Theologen* (Leipzig 1898).

961

Hausherr, Irénée 'L'hésychasme. Etude de spiritualité' *Orientalia christiana periodica* 22 (1956) 5-40, 247-85.

962

Meyendorff, John *Byzantine Hesychasm: Historical, Theological and Social Problems* (Variorum Reprint Collected Studies Series 26; London 1974)

Collected articles. Not seen.

963

Hausherr, Irénée *Saint Théodore Studite. L'homme et l'ascète (d'après ses catéchèses)* (Orientalia christiana [analecta] 6.1; Rome 1926)

Cf **120**.

964

Lot-Borodine, Myrrha *Un maître de la spiritualité byzantine au XIVe siècle. Nicolas Cabasilas* (Paris 1958)

Cf also Sévérien Salaville in *Etudes byzantines* 1 (1943) 5-57.

RUSSIAN

965

Fedotov, Georgiĭ P. *The Russian Religious Mind* 2 vols (Cambridge, Mass. 1946-66)

Vol I: Kievan Christianity (tenth to thirteenth centuries); II: Middle Ages (thirteenth to fifteenth centuries).

LATE MIDDLE AGES

966

Vandenbroucke, François *Pour l'histoire de la théologie morale. La morale*

monastique du XIe au XVIe siècle (Analecta mediaevalia namurcensia 20; Louvain - Lille 1966)
Brief biographies and accounts of the works of leading Benedictines, Cistercians, and Carthusians.

967
Grundmann, Herbert *Religiöse Bewegungen im Mittelalter. Untersuchungen über die geschichtlichen Zusammenhänge zwischen der Ketzerei, den Bettelorden und der religiösen Frauenbewegung im 12. und 13. Jahrhundert und über die geschichtlichen Grundlagen der deutschen Mystik* (Historische Studien, ed Ebering, 267; Berlin 1935; repr with 'Neue Beiträge zur Geschichte der religiösen Bewegungen im Mittelalter' [1955], 1961).

968
Roisin, Simone *L'hagiographie cistercienne dans le diocèse de Liège au XIIIe siècle* (Université de Louvain: Recueil de travaux d'histoire et de philologie, 3 S, 27; Louvain - Brussels 1947)
On the ideal of monastic perfection.

969
Pre-Reformation English Spirituality ed James Walsh (London - New York 1965)
20 articles on writers from Bede to Augustine Baker, including Edmund Colledge on 'Early English Religious Literature' (pp 15-38).

970
Histoire spirituelle de la France. Spiritualité du catholicisme en France et dans les pays du langue française des origines à 1914 (= *Dictionnaire de spiritualité* **41**, V, 785-1004; Paris 1964)
Includes sections on Christian antiquity (Jacques Fontaine), early Middle Ages (Pierre Riché), monastic spirituality (Jean Leclercq), thirteenth and fourteenth centuries (Edmond-René Labande), and fifteenth century (Francis Rapp).

971
Lohse, Bernhard *Mönchtum und Reformation. Luthers Auseinandersetzung mit dem Mönchsideal des Mittelalters* (Forschungen zur Kirchen- und Dogmengeschichte 12; Göttingen 1963)
Includes sections on the ascetic and monastic ideals of the early church and selected medieval writers.

IMAGE OF MONASTICISM IN VERNACULAR POETRY

972
Scheuten, Paul *Das Mönchtum in der altfranzösischen Profandichtung (12.-14. Jahrhundert)* (Beiträge 7; Münster W. 1921).
973
Schneider, Rudolf *Der Mönch in der englischen Dichtung bis auf Lewis's 'Monk' 1795* (Palaestra 155; Leipzig 1928).

CONCEPT OF MONASTIC LIFE

974
Morin, Germain *L'idéal monastique et la vie chrétienne des premiers jours* (1912) 4th ed (Collection pax 3; Maredsous 1927; Eng trans by C. Gunning 1914).
975
Leclercq, Jean *La vie parfaite. Points de vue sur l'essence de l'état religieux* (Turnhout - Paris 1948; Eng trans 1961).
976
Leclercq, Jean *Etudes sur le vocabulaire monastique du moyen âge* (Stud Ans 48; Rome 1961)
Studies *monachus, philosophia, theoria*.
977
Leclercq, Jean *Otia monastica. Etudes sur le vocabulaire de la contemplation au moyen âge* (Stud Ans 51; Rome 1963)
Studies *quies, otium, vacatio, sabbatum*.
978
Emonds, Hilarius 'Geistlicher Kriegsdienst. Der Topos der *militia spiritualis* in der antiken Philosophie' *Heilige Überlieferung* (826) 21-50.
979
Malone, Edward E. 'Martyrdom and Monastic Profession as a Second Baptism' *Vom christlichen Mysterium* 835, 115-34; and 'The Monk and the Martyr' in *Antonius Magnus* 92, 201-28
Cf 1026.
980
Hilpisch, Stephanus 'Das benediktinisch-monastische Ideal im Wandel der Zeiten' *Stud Mitt* 68 (1957) 73-85; Eng trans in *American Benedictine Review* 15 (1964) 381-94.

981
Colombás, García M. 'El concepto de monje y vida monástica hasta fines del siglo V' *Stud mon* 1 (1959) 257-342; partial Eng trans in *Monastic Studies* 2 (1964) 65-117.

982
Penco, Gregorio 'Il concetto di monaco e di vita monastica in Occidente nel secolo VI' *Stud mon* 1 (1959) 7-50.

983
Ranke-Heinemann, Uta *Das frühe Mönchtum. Seine Motive nach den Selbstzeugnissen* (Essen 1964) Chapters on love of God, desire for death, search for perfection, fight against demons, angelic life, etc.

Angelic Life

Cf 983.

984
Severus, Emmanuel von ' "Bios angelikos". Zum Verständnis des Mönchslebens als "Engelleben" in der christlichen Überlieferung' *Die Engel in der Welt und Heute* ed Theodor Bogler (Liturgie und Mönchtum 21; Maria Laach 1957) 56-70.

985
Frank, Karl Suso ΑΓΓΑΛΙΚΟΣ ΒΙΟΣ. *Begriffsanalytische und begriffsgeschichtliche Untersuchung zum 'engelgleichen Leben' im frühen Mönchtum* (Beiträge 26; Münster W. 1964).

986
Penco, Gregorio 'L'imitazione di Cristo nell'agiografia monastica' *Coll cist* 28 (1966) 17-34.

987
Biffi, Inos 'Aspetti dell'imitazione de Cristo nella letteratura monastica del secolo XII' *La scuola cattolica* 96 (1968) 451-90.

Apostolic Life

988
Frank, Karl Suso 'Vita apostolica. Ansätze zur apostolischen Lebensform in der alten Kirche' *Zs für KG* 82 (1971) 145-66.

989

Vicaire, Marie-Humbert *L'imitation des apôtres. Moines, chanoines et mendiants, IVe-XIIIe siècles* (Tradition et spiritualité 2; Paris 1963).

990

McDonnell, Ernest W. 'The "Vita apostolica": Diversity or Dissent' *Church History* 24 (1955) 15-31.

FLIGHT FROM THE WORLD

991

Baur, Chrysostomus 'Der weltflüchtige und welttätige Gedanke in der Entwicklung des Mönchtums' *Bonner Zs für Theologie und Seelsorge* 7 (1930) 113-26.

992

Gribomont, Jean 'Le renoncement au monde dans l'idéal ascétique de Saint Basile' *Irénikon* 31 (1958) 282-307, 460-75.

993

Winandy, Jacques 'L'idée de fuite du monde dans la tradition monastique' *Le message des moines à notre temps* (Paris 1958) 95-104.

CONTEMPT FOR THE WORLD

994

Bultot, Robert *Christianisme et valeurs humaines*, A: *La doctrine du mépris du monde en Occident de S Ambroise à Innocent III.*, IV: *Le XIe siècle* 2 vols (Louvain - Paris 1963-4)
Vol I: Peter Damiani; II: John of Fécamp, Hermanus Contractus, Roger of Caen, Anselm of Canterbury.

995

Grégoire, Réginald 'Saeculi actibus se facere alienum. Le "mépris du monde" dans la littérature monastique latine médiévale' *Revue d'ascétique et de mystique* 41 (1965) 251-87
With a note by Jean Leclercq (pp 287-90).

996

Lazzari, Francesco *Il 'contemptus mundi' nella scuola di S Vittore* (Naples 1965)
Cf Robert Bultot in *Revue des sciences philosophiques et théologiques* 51 (1967) 3-22, and Louis-Jacques Bataillon and Jean Pierre Jossua *ibid* 23-38, with a bibliography on this topic.

997

Lazzari, Francesco *Monachesimo e valori umani tra XI e XII secolo* (Milan - Naples 1969)

Collected articles.

FRIENDSHIP

998

Fiske, Adele M. *Friends and Friendship in the Monastic Tradition* (Cuernavaca 1970)

Collected articles. Not seen.

POVERTY

Cf **332, 670**.

999

Dmitrewski, Michael von *Die christliche freiwillige Armut vom Ursprung der Kirche bis zum 12. Jahrhundert* (Berlin - Leipzig 1913).

1000

Bligny, Bernard 'Les premiers Chartreux et la pauvreté' *Le Moyen Âge* 57 (4 S, 6; 1951) 27-60.

1001

Durand, Jean *Vie commune et pauvreté chez les religieux* (Montreal - Paris 1952).

1002

Povertà e ricchezza nella spiritualità dei secoli XI e XII (Convegni del Centro di studi sulla spiritualità medievale 8; Todi 1969)

Cf Gabriella Severino in *Bullettino dell'Istituto storico italiano per il medio evo* 79 (1968) 149-65.

1003

Grégoire, Réginald 'La place de la pauvreté dans la conception et la pratique de la vie monastique médiévale latine' *Monachesimo* **221**, 173-92.

1004

Witters, Willibrord 'Pauvres et pauvreté dans les coutumiers monastiques de moyen âge' *Etudes sur l'histoire de la pauvreté* ed Michel Mollat (Publications de la Sorbonne: Série 'Etudes' 8; Paris 1974) [I] 177-215.

WORK

Cf 814.

1005

Levasseur, Emile 'Le travail des moines dans les monastères' *Séances et travaux de l'Académie des sciences morales et politiques* 154 (NS, 60; 1900) 449-70.

1006

Redonet y López Dóriga, Luis *El trabajo manual en las reglas monásticas* (Madrid 1919)
With a 'Contestación' by Adolfo Bonilla y San Martín.

1007

Dörries, Hermann 'Mönchtum und Arbeit' *Forschungen zur Kirchengeschichte und zur christlichen Kunst (Festschrift Johannes Ficker)* (Leipzig 1931) 17-39 and *Wort und Stunde* 132, I, 277-301
Concentrates on Eastern monasticism.

1008

Warren, Henry B. de 'Le travail manuel chez les moines à travers les âges' *La vie spirituelle* 52 (1937) *Supplément* [80]-[123]
Not seen.

1009

Delaruelle, Etienne 'Le travail dans les règles monastiques occidentales du quatrième au neuvième siècle' *Journal de psychologie normale et pathologique* 41 (1948) 51-62
With discussion involving Marc Bloch (pp 63-4).

PEREGRINATION

1010

Campenhausen, Hans von *Die asketische Heimatslosigkeit im altkirchlichen und frühmittelalterlichen Mönchtum* (Sammlung gemeinverständlicher Vorträge und Schriften aus dem Gebiet der Theologie und Religionsgeschichte 149; Tübingen 1930).

1011

Leclercq, Jean 'Mönchtum und Peregrinatio im Frühmittelalter' *Römische Quartalschrift für christliche Altertumskunde und Kirchengeschichte* 55 (1960) 212-25; and 'Monachisme et pérégrination du IXe au XIIe siècle' *Stud mon* 3 (1961) 33-52; both reprinted in *Sources* 946.

1012

Guillaumont, Antoine 'Le dépaysement comme forme d'ascèse, dans le monachisme ancien' *Ecole pratique des hautes études, V^e section - Sciences religieuses: Annuaire* 76 (1968-9) 31-58.

ASCETICISM

Cf **64, 68, 116, 120, 168.**

1013

Zöckler, Otto *Askese und Mönchtum* (1863) 2nd ed 2 vols paged consecutively (Frankfurt 1897)
First edition entitled *Kritischen Geschichte der Askese.*

1014

Berlière, Ursmer *L'ascèse bénédictine des origines à la fin du XIIe siècle* (Collection pax in-8°, 1; Paris - Maredsous 1927).

1015

Buonaiuti, Ernesto *Le origini dell'ascetismo cristiano* (Pinerolo 1928)
Covers from pre-Christian to fourth century.

1016

Viller, Marcel and Karl Rahner *Aszese und Mystik in der Väterzeit* (Freiburg B. 1939)
Based on Viller's *La spiritualité des premiers siècles chrétiens* (1930).

1017

Stolz, Anselme *L'ascèse chrétienne* (Irénikon, NS, 2; Chevetogne 1948).

1018

Salmon, Pierre 'L'ascèse monastique et la spiritualité' *La vie spirituelle: Supplément* 7 (1954) 195-240.

1019

Kretschmar, Georg 'Ein Beitrag zur Frage nach dem Ursprung frühchristlicher Askese' *Zs für Theologie und Kirche* 61 (1964) 27-67.

1020

Turbessi, Giuseppe *Ascetismo e monachesimo prebenedettino* (Universale studium 78; Rome 1961); and *Ascetismo e monachesimo in S Benedetto* (Universale studium 101; Rome 1965).

1021

Nagel, Peter *Die Motivierung der Askese in der alten Kirche und der Ursprung des Mönchtums* (Texte und Untersuchungen zur Geschichte der altchristlichen Literatur 95; Berlin 1966).

1022

Bickel, Ernst 'Das asketische Ideal bei Ambrosius, Hieronymus und Augustin. Eine kulturgeschichtliche Studie' *Neue Jahrbücher für das klassische Altertum, Geschichte und deutsche Literatur und für Pädagogik* 37 (1916) 437-74.

1023

Il dolore e la morte nella spiritualità dei secoli XII e XIII (Convegni del Centro di studi sulla spiritualità medievale 5; Todi 1967) Includes articles on the theme of sadness and death in art and literature.

1024

Lohse, Bernhard *Askese und Mönchtum in der Antike und in der alten Kirche* (Religion und Kultur der alten Mittelmeerwelt in Parallelforschungen 1; Munich - Vienna 1969).

1025

Schmeidler, Bernhard 'Anti-asketische Äusserungen aus Deutschlands im 11. und beginnenden 12. Jahrhundert' *Kultur und Universalgeschichte (Festschrift Walter Goetz)* (Leipzig - Berlin 1927) 35-52.

DEVOTIONS

1026

Gougaud, Louis *Dévotions et pratiques ascétiques du moyen âge* (Collection pax 21; Paris - Maredsous 1925; revised Eng trans by G. C. Bateman 1927) See **776** and articles on prayer, fasting, immersion, flagellation, desire for martyrdom, etc.

1027

Musurillo, Herbert 'The Problem of Ascetical Fasting in the Greek Patristic Writers' *Traditio* 12 (1956) 1-64.

1028

Berlière, Ursmer *La dévotion au Sacré-Coeur dans l'ordre de S Benoît* (Collection pax 10; Paris - Maredsous 1923).

1029

Schäfer, Thomas *Die Fusswaschung im monastischen Brauchtum und in der lateinischen Liturgie* (Texte und Arbeiten herausgegeben durch die Erzabtei Beuron I, 47; Beuron 1956).

1030

Dörries, Hermann 'The Place of Confession in Ancient Monasticism' *Studia patristica: Papers Presented to the Third International Conference*

on *Patristic Studies held at Christ Church, Oxford, 1959,* III (Texte und Untersuchungen zur Geschichte der altchristlichen Literatur 80; Berlin 1962) 284-311
Also published in German in 1960 and in *Wort und Stunde* 132, I, 225-50.

1031
Penco, Gregorio 'Forme ascetiche e pratiche penitenziali nella tradizione monastica' *Bollettino della Deputazione di storia patria per l'Umbria* 64.2 (1967) 334-52.

VIRTUES AND VICES

1032
Raasch, Juana 'The Monastic Conception of Purity of Heart and its Sources' *Stud mon* 8 (1966) 7-33, 183-213; 10 (1968) 7-55; 11 (1969) 269-314; 12 (1970) 7-41
Early monasticism through the fourth century.

1033
Dingjan, François *Discretio. Les origines patristiques et monastiques de la doctrine sur la prudence chez Saint Thomas d'Aquin* (Van Gorcum's Theologische Bibliotheek 38; Assen 1967)
Cassian, Benedict, Gregory, Bernard, Hugh and Richard of St Victor, etc.

1034
Bacht, Heinrich ' "Meditatio" in den ältesten Mönchsquellen' *Geist und Leben* 28 (1955) 360-73.

1035
Gómez, Alberto 'Compunctio lacrymarum. Doctrina de la compunción en el monacato latino de los siglos IV-VI' *Coll cist* 23 (1961) 232-53.

1036
Wenzel, Siegfried ' "Acedia" 700-1200 ' *Traditio* 22 (1966) 73-102; and *The Sin of Sloth: Acedia in Medieval Thought and Literature* (Chapel Hill 1967).

Index of Authors and Editors

All references are to entry numbers, not to pages.

Toronto Medieval Bibliographies

Editor: John Leyerle
Director, Centre for Medieval Studies, University of Toronto

1
Old Norse-Icelandic Studies
Hans Bekker-Nielsen, Editor, *Mediaeval Scandinavia*, Co-editor of
Bibliography of Old Norse-Icelandic Studies and of *Den Arnamagnæanske
Kommissions Ordbog*, Odense University

2
Old English Literature
Fred C. Robinson, Department of English, Yale University

3
Medieval Rhetoric
James J. Murphy, Chairman, Department of Rhetoric,
University of California (Davis)

4
Medieval Music: The Sixth Liberal Art
Andrew Hughes, Faculty of Music, University of Toronto

5
Medieval Celtic Literature
Rachel Bromwich, University Reader in Celtic Languages and Literature,
University of Cambridge

6
Medieval Monasticism
Giles Constable, Henry Charles Lea Professor of Medieval History,
Harvard University

In preparation

Aids to the Study of Literary History
Richard H. Rouse, Department of History, University of California
(Los Angeles)

Arthurian Legend and Romance
Edmund Reiss, Department of English, Duke University

Chaucer
John Leyerle, Director, Centre for Medieval Studies, University of Toronto

Italian Literature to 1400
John Freccero, Department of Romance Languages, Yale University, and
Giuseppe Mazzotta, Department of Romance Studies, Cornell University

Latin Palaeography to 1500
Leonard E. Boyle, OP, Pontifical Institute of Mediaeval Studies, Toronto

Medieval Exact Science and Natural Philosophy
John E. Murdoch, Chairman, Department of the History of Science,
Harvard University

Medieval Latin Literature
A. G. Rigg, Centre for Medieval Studies, University of Toronto

Medieval Materia Medica and Applied Botany
Jerry Stannard, Department of History, University of Kansas

Medieval Scots Poetry
Florence H. Ridley, Department of English, University of California
(Los Angeles)

Middle English Literature
L. D. Benson, Department of English, Harvard University

Middle High German Literature
R. William Leckie, Jr, Department of German, University College,
University of Toronto

Old Provençal
Robert A. Taylor, Department of French, Victoria College,
University of Toronto

Sources and Methodology for the Interpretation of Medieval Imagery
R. E. Kaske, Department of English, Cornell University

Spanish Literature to 1500
James F. Burke, Department of Italian and Hispanic Studies, University of
Toronto, and John E. Keller, Director, School of Letters and Languages,
University of Kentucky